# BITS and PIECES

**51 Activities
for Teaching Japanese
K–12**

Distributed in the United States by Kodansha America, Inc., 114 Fifth Avenue, New York N.Y. 10011, and in the United Kingdom and continental Europe by Kodansha Europe Ltd., 95 Aldwych, London WC2B 4JF. Published by Kodansha International Ltd., 17-14 Otowa 1-chome, Bunkyo-ku, Tokyo 112, and Kodansha America, Inc.

First edition, 1997

97 98 99 00 10 9 8 7 6 5 4 3 2 1

ISBN 4-7700-2029-5

# BITS
## and
# PIECES

## 51 Activities for Teaching Japanese K–12

日本語教材 ● アクティビティ集

Japanese Council of International Schools

KODANSHA INTERNATIONAL
Tokyo · New York · London

# Contents

## The Activities

# FOREWORD

Several years after moving to Hong Kong with my family, my young daughter, Rebecca, rushed in from school one day and cried, "Daddy, Daddy, I know how to talk Putonghua." "Really?" I replied. "Sure," she said. She then proceeded to say, "Hello. My name's Rebecca. What's your name?" in Putonghua. Her delight at being able to use another language to communicate, at however a rudimentary a level, was obvious. There is magic in language, and Rebecca had clearly been enchanted by the ability to express herself in a language that was not her own.

This evening, as I sat down to write this introductory piece, Rebecca came home from school and threw her books onto the dining table. "What's the matter?" I asked. "Putonghua," she said. "That's the matter." What had happened to Rebecca and her magical excursions into language learning in the years between her initial contact with Putonghua and today?

The answer, I'm afraid, is the educational process. Rebecca's first teacher had been young, enthusiastic, and innovative. She showed her young learners the excitement and magic in language learning by making connections between the language and their own lives. Unfortunately, this teacher left the school, and the teacher who replaced her subscribed to the decontextualized view of learning, in which the acquisition of a second language consists of the manipulation and rote learning of abstract grammatical, lexical, and phonological symbols that make minimal contact with the lives of the learners. It is a matter of deep regret, but hardly a cause for wonder, that the magic of language learning had disappeared from Rebecca's pedagogical existence.

It is an unfortunate fact that most teachers (and therefore learners) see the acquisition of another language as a war of attrition. "If it isn't causing you pain, then you aren't doing it right," as a teacher of mine once told me. Study after study demonstrates that formal instruction is, more often than not, accompanied by the sort of steady decrease in motivation that I observed in my daughter.

And yet, must a decrease in interest and motivation inevitably accompany the educational process? My own experience as an educator and teacher in many different cultural contexts over a considerable number of years leads me to think that it need not. If the learning process can connect the educational experience with the experiential reality of the learner, then interest and motivation can actually be enhanced. The ingredients that foster such interest and motivation can all be found within the learners themselves.

In short, if learners can see the point, and if the tasks themselves are worth doing for their own sake, then the learners will want to be involved. It was the desire to develop tasks that were consistent with these ideas that led Yuri Kite and her colleagues to put together this collection. I find it flattering that my own work in learner-centered education should have been an inspiration.

What is learner-centered teaching? The essential feature is that the learners themselves are personally involved in their own learning. This concept has two dimensions. First is the notion that learners can have some say in what they want to learn and how they want to go about learning it. This involves taking a long view of education, and learners need a considerable period of sensitization to the learning process before they can make informed decisions. Basically, they need to learn what it means to be a learner. The second dimension of learner-centeredness can help to foster such sensitivity. This view sees learners as the ones who actually do the work in the classroom. Through engagement and personally relevant task-based activities, learners are involved in structuring and restructuring their understanding of, and ability to use, the target language. In short, they are involved in learning through doing.

The learner-centered notion of learning through doing, which underpins *Bits and Pieces*, has come into language education from the world of humanistic psychology and experiential learning. In experiential learning, the learner's immediate personal experiences are taken as the point of departure for deciding how to organize the learning process. Proponents of experiential learning dispute the notion that teaching is a matter of handing on knowledge from one generation to another, and they reject the idea that knowledge is some kind of commodity to be bartered in intellectual trading places known as schools and universities. Rather, they embrace the notion that the essential function of education is to facilitate the process whereby learners make their own meanings. The assertion that "If students are to learn, then they must ultimately do the learning for themselves" is an apt summation of their belief.

While it is important that tasks be interesting and enjoyable for learners, that is not enough. They must also be interesting and enjoyable for the teacher. In developing *Bits and Pieces*, the authors were very much aware that good materials, in addition to facilitating more effective and more enjoyable learning, should also make the teacher's work easier and more meaningful.

Finally, I would like to congratulate all those who have been involved in the evolution of the book (an evolution that I have followed with interest over the past two or three years) and to say how pleased I am to have been associated with the project.

David Nunan<br>
The University of Hong Kong<br>
August 1977

# Bits and Pieces によせて

　数年前、家族で香港に引っ越してきて間もなくのころ、娘のレベッカが学校から帰ってくるなり声を張り上げて「ねえパパ、あたしPutonghua（普通話）ができるんだから」というのです。私が「本当？」というと、娘は「うん」というなり「こんにちは、わたしの名はレベッカ、あなたのお名前は？」とPutonghuaでしゃべり出しました。それがどんなに未熟なものであって、母国語以外のことばでコミュニケーションができたという娘の喜びは私にもひしひしと伝わってきました。ことばというものには不思議な力があるもので、レベッカは外国のことばでコミュニケーションできるということにすっかり有頂天になっていたのです。

　ところが、ちょうどこの文章を書いていたとき、学校から戻ったレベッカはいきなり教科書をテーブルに投げだしました。なにか問題でもあったのかと尋ねると、Putonghuaが問題だと言い出しました。あれほど夢中になって勉強していたのに、いつの間にこんなことになってしまったのでしょうか。

　答えは教え方にあることが分かりました。レベッカの最初の先生というのは、若くて教育熱心、そして進取の気象に富んだ人でした。授業では、生徒たちが経験する日々の出来事とことばがいかに密接に結びついているかを示し、ことばが本来持っている不思議さや楽しさを生徒たちに教えたのでした。

　しかし生憎その先生が去り、後任の先生がやってきたわけです。大変残念なのですが、この人は第二言語を習得するということを、実際の生活とはほとんど没交渉の、文法上、音韻学上あるいは辞書上の抽象的概念をただ機械的に覚えたり、手際よく処理したりすることにあるといった考えの持ち主だったのです。これではレベッカが学習をとおして味わったことばの魅力など吹き飛んでしまうのも無理ありません。

　また語学教育の世界では、残念ながらほとんどの教師が、（ということは生徒たちも）外国語学習を疲れ果てるまでやる泥試合のように考えてしまっていることです。「勉強していて辛いと感じないなら、君の勉強のしかたが悪いのだ」と私はある先生に言われたことがあります。しかし次から次へ出てくる研究が示しているように従来型の学習法、文脈や背景を無視して機械的に勉強させるやり方では、大抵の場合学習意欲がそがれることになります。現に娘のレベッカを見ていてもそうなのです。

　それでは勉強をしていく過程で、興味や動機が薄れてしまうのは避けがたいものなのでしょうか。私は、長年いろいろな文化的環境のなかで教育者としてまた教師としてやってきましたが、必ずしもそうではないと考えるようになりました。もし生徒たちが生活のなかで体験する実感をうまく反映させるような教え方ができれば、薄れるどころか、逆に高められるものであり、その力は学習者自身に備わったものだと思うのです。

　要するに学習者は学習のポイントがはっきりしていて、そのタスクがやりがいのあるものなら、すすんで参加したいと考えるでしょう。そうした要求を満たすタスクを開発することこそ望ましいことであり、カイト由利子氏および執筆者の方々がこのアクティビティ集で試みようとしていることもまさにそれなのです。それにしましても、私の学習者中心の言語学習教育が本書になにがしかのアイデアを提供したということを知り、大変嬉しく感じている次第です。

ところで、学習者中心の言語学習ですが、この基本は学習者が単にクラスの中の一人として授業を受けるのではなく、あくまでも主人公として学習に臨むところにあります。そこでこの学習法が2つの面をもつことを説明したいのですが、ひとつは学習者中心ということですから、生徒は学習内容や方法に対してある程度自分たちの希望を容れてもらえます。ですがやはり実際には長い学習経験がなければこうしたことに意見をいうのはなかなかむつかしく、またしっかりした判断をくだすには、自分がどのようにして学んできたのか、学習の経緯といったものを認識するある程度の時間が必要となるわけです。つまり学習者自身、学習者とはどういうものであるか自覚をしなければいけないということになります。その自覚を促すものが、この学習法のもう一つの面、学習者をアクティビティに参加させるタスク学習です。授業に積極的に参加し、自分を表現するかたちでアクティビティに取り組むことで、学習者は学ぶべき目標言語に対する理解を整理、再確認し、またそれらを実際に使う能力を養っていくことになります。要するに、生徒たちは自ら行うことで学ぶということに深く係わるわけです。

　本書 Bits and Pieces の柱でもある、学習者中心のタスク学習の考え方は、ヒューマニスティック心理学や体験学習の世界から語学教育の分野にもたらされたものなのですが体験学習では、学習者の個人的体験は学習プロセスを作成するための出発点として扱われます。この学習法の支持者は、知識とは世代から世代へと渡されるものだという見方に異を唱えるとともに、知のマーケットとでもいえる学校や大学で商品のごとく売り買いされるものだという考え方を否定しています。彼らの考え方では、教育の基本的機能とはそれぞれの学習者が自律的に学んでゆくそのプロセスを facilitate（促進）することに他ならないということなのです。その主張を煎じ詰めれば「学習しようと思っている人は、自分たち自身で学んでいかねばならない」ということになるでしょう。

　しかしタスクは、学習者だけがおもしろがったり、楽しかったりするだけでは十分とはいえません。教える側にとっても同様におもしろく、楽しくあるべきなのです。 Bits and Pieces の執筆陣は、優れた教材というものが、学習効果を高め、勉強をより楽しくするのみならず、教師の仕事をも楽に、また意味のあるものにするということを十分に踏まえて本書を作り上げています。

　最後になりましたが、この数年間、本書の開発を興味をもって見守ってきた者としまして、その開発に当たられた全てのみなさまにお祝いを申し上げたいと思います。またこのプロジェクトの一端に加えていただけたことを大変うれしく思っております。

1997年8月
デイヴィッド・ヌーナン
（香港大学）

# PREFACE

*Bits and Pieces* is a book of classroom activities to be used as supplementary material in the teaching of beginner-level and intermediate Japanese. In particular, this book is aimed at teachers who are about to start or who have just started teaching Japanese. With young students, if classes are not interesting, they often learn very little, and if the class is downright boring, they simply stop paying attention. The challenge for teachers is to make the class have relevance to their students. All the ideas in this book are suggestions to help you, the teacher, meet this challenge.

This book can help you with your teaching no matter what the curriculum or the syllabus you are working with. Some of the activities in this book are five-minute warming-up activities to be used at the start of class to get your students going. Other activities described here will take up the whole lesson. In short, there is something here for everybody and for every situation.

The point that should perhaps be stressed the most in this introduction is to use this book flexibly, tailoring the activities described here to suit the age and level of your students. *Bits and Pieces* is the fruit of many teachers' work and experience teaching Japanese over a period of many years. No doubt some of the activities will need to be adapted to fit the requirements and abilities of your classes and the restrictions on time and space you have to work in. Please adapt them however you see fit.

The philosophy that has guided us as we wrote *Bits and Pieces* is the task-based instruction and learner-centeredness in language learning advocated by scholars such as David Nunan (1988, 1989). It is our sincere hope that the teaching of Japanese is slowly working towards the adoption of a curriculum where the needs and wants of the students are given priority.

Yuriko Kite
August 1997

## Explanation of the Headings

### AIMS OF THE ACTIVITY:
The purpose and goal of the activity is given based on the notion of learning strategies (Nunan 1989, Oxford 1990) or goals specific to Japanese expressions or grammar (e.g., practicing ~*te*).

### IMPORTANT EXPRESSIONS:
Words, expressions, and points of grammar to be studied in the course of the activity are specified here.

### LEVEL OF JAPANESE:
For the sake of convenience we have specified the students' level of Japanese. There are three levels—beginners, intermediate, and advanced—based on the number of hours of study completed. Do not be overly concerned about these levels, but choose activities that seem to you to best suit your students' needs. The levels below are given merely as a rough guide:

| | |
|---|---|
| Beginners | (0–180 hours of study) |
| Intermediate | (180–270 hours of study) |
| Advanced | (more than 270 hours of study) |

### STUDENTS' AGE:
Approximate age groups are given for convenience sake; they should not be considered restrictive. They are 6 to 8, 6 to 10, 6 to 13, 8 to 10, 8 to 13, 8 to 18, 11 to 13, 11 to 18, 14 to 18, and all ages.

### REQUIRED TIME:
An estimate of the time it takes to complete the activity.

### WHAT THE STUDENTS MUST ALREADY KNOW:
The bare minimum of background knowledge needed for the successful completion of the activity.

### MATERIALS TO PREPARE:
The things you will need to prepare before carrying out the activity (excluding those things that are normally found in a classroom anyway). There are some items that will require virtually no time at all to get ready, and others that will have to be prepared well in advance.

### PROCEDURE:
The steps needed for the successful completion of the activity are given here.

### ADVICE FOR THE TEACHER:
Hints and suggestions from experienced teachers in the field on how to make the activities go successfully and how to adapt them to suit your students' needs.

### APPENDIX:
Almost all the material provided at the back of the book can be photocopied and used in class with no further preparation time necessary.

**REFERENCE:**

Nunan, David. *The Learner-Centered Curriculum.* Cambridge University Press, 1988.

Nunan, David. *Designing Tasks for the Communicative Classroom.* Cambridge University Press, 1989.

Oxford, Rebecca L. *Language Learning Strategies: What Every Teacher Should Know.* Heinle and Heinle, 1990.

## Acknowledgments and Credits

**PROJECT COORDINATOR**

Dr. Yuriko K. Kite — Canadian Academy

**EDITING TEAM**

Dr. Suzuko Nishihara — The National Language Research Institute

Noriko Hayashi — Nishimachi International School

Sachiko Inoh — St. Mary's International School

Akiko Otagaki — Osaka International School

Chie Scoggins — St. Maur International School

Sumiko Shimizu — St. Mary's International School

Sachiko Riley — St. Joseph International School

Koshizu Tanaka — The American School in Japan

Tamako Ueda — International School of the Sacred Heart

**ADVISORS**

Dr. Toshio Okazaki — Tsukuba University

Dr. Tazuko Uyeno — Tokyo Woman's Christian University

Dr. Suzuko Nishihara — The National Language Research Institute

**ARTWORK CONSULTANT**

Tom Roberts — Canadian Academy

**SUPPORTING STAFF**

Hiroko Aizawa — The American School in Japan

Chieko Hasamune

Yoshiko Kasai

Noriko Matsumoto

Maki Moriyama

Wako Naoi

Hasami Shimba

Koshizu Tanaka

Hiroko Taira — The British School in Tokyo

Hiroko Furumoto — Canadian Academy

Fumiko Ito

Yoshiko Kawabata

Fujiko Otani

Michiko Senoh

Hisano Richeson

Junko Iwabuchi — Christian Academy in Japan

Tamako Miyagi — Hiroshima International School

Misa Kawanaka — International School of the Sacred Heart

Tamako Ueda

Yasuko Seo — Japan International School

Himiko Obayashi

Sachiko Kobayashi — Kansai Christian School

Nishimachi International School Team — Nishimachi International School

Nakae Osako — Osaka International School

Akiko Otagaki

Ryosuke Nakamura

Ayumi Kita — St. Joseph International School

Sachiko Riley

Mayumi Hayaki — St. Maur International School

Chizuko Ii

Junko Matsuda

Kazuko Momomi

Chie Scoggins

Masumi Ichikawa Naylor — Seisen International School

Kyoko Miyagi — Sendai American School

Sachiko Inou — St. Mary's International School

Br. Philippe Ozawa

Chiyoko Sakurai
Sumiko Shimizu
Keiko Toki
Tamiko Usyak
Yoshiomi Yasunari
Hiromi Akasaki       St. Michael's International
                              School

Tazu Makino
Masako Okazaki
Kazumi Kinouchi       Yokohama International
                                School

Michiko Takeda
Sachiko Yanagawa
Naoko Unno

---

## Acknowledgments (random order)

The Ishibashi Foundation, Michihiko Ushijima and Keiko Nakano (The Japan Forum), Dr. David Nunan (The University of Hong Kong), Dr. Seiichi Makino (Princeton University), Dr. Osamu Kamada (Kyoto University of Foreign Studies), James L. Wiese (formerly Osaka International School), Br. Michel Jutras (St. Mary's International School), Dr. Leila Metcalf (Canadian Academy), Sue Hale (The American School in Japan), JCIS Headmasters and Headmistresses, Japanese Language Project Steering Committee, Japanese language teachers of JCIS, Keiko Yoneyama and Atsuko Mosser (Canadian Academy), Hiroko Fukuda (Shohoku College), Michael Brase and Shigeyoshi Suzuki (Kodansha International).

# まえがき

　Bits and Pieces は、主に初等、中等教育レベルを対象にした日本語教育のための副教材です。これから日本語を教えようとする先生方、まだ教え始めたばかりで経験の浅い先生方などが教室で役立てていただけるよう工夫してあります。

　生徒たちに教える場合、内容の問題もさることながら、いかに教えるかということが常に重要な問題となります。特に学習者が年少者の場合、教え方が悪ければ、たちまち関心を失い、大人のように我慢して耳を傾けてはくれません。教師たちに求められることは、いかにして学習者の興味を喚起し、学習効果を上げるかということにあるといえるでしょう。本書は、生徒たちと先生方が一体となって楽しめ、かつ自然に学習効果が伴うようなアクティビティを集めたものです。

　副教材に求められることは、どのようなカリキュラム、授業形態、学習教材にも柔軟に対応でき、かつ学習者のレベルや年齢に応じた広い選択肢を持つことだと思います。本書で扱ったアクティビティはどれも、長い間日本語教育にたずさわってきた私たちの経験、教育現場の中から生まれてきたものです。学習者の理解度や関心、教材の種類、アクティビティに要する時間や場所、人数などについてできるだけ実践的で細かな配慮を加えたつもりです。例えば、あるアクティビティは本格的にクラスを始める前のウォーミングアップ用として5分間くらいで効率よくできるようになっていますし、またあるものは授業時間すべてを費やしてやるよう構成されています。同一のアクティビティであってもプロセスを簡略化したり、あるいは追加したりして臨機応変に授業に取り入れられるよう随所に具体的なサジェスチョンを付しました。ですから実際に本書を使って授業を行う場合には、状況やニーズに応じてアクティビティを選んでいただき、また必要があれば積極的にそれぞれの場に合わせて変えていっていただきたいと思います。

　Bits and Pieces は、デイヴィッド・ヌーナン氏などの提唱するタスク学習、つまり学習者中心の言語学習に基づくものです。日本語教育における学校の教育理念、教師の信念、カリキュラム、授業の形態などそれぞれ一つ一つ (bits and pieces) が、学習者中心の言語学習となって芽を出し、力強く成長して欲しいという願いが込められたものです。それぞれの教育現場でこの新しい芽が育まれることを祈って止みません。

1997年8月<br>
カイト由利子

# 見出しの説明

## ● アクティビティのねらい

学習ストラテジー(Nunan, 1989, Oxford, 1990) に基づいたアクティビティの目的（例：「音と文字システムをきちんと練習する」）、また具体的な学習課題（例：五七五のシラブルでリズムとともに主語＋目的語＋述語の語順を学ぶ）を示している。アクティビティのねらいを明らかにすることにより、アクティビティの使い方や進め方あるいは学習評価などに役立つ。

## 重要な表現

アクティビティで学習する単語、表現、文法など。アクティビティが、学習項目によって応用できる場合には、特に記していない（例えばビンゴなどは、文字、場所、動物の名前など自由に変えることができる）。

## 学習者の日本語レベル

便宜上、学習時間によっては次の3段階に分けているが、このレベルにあまりこだわらず、アクティビティの内容を見て判断してほしい。参考までに、学習者のレベルを示しておく。

    初級（入門・中・上）    （0時間～180時間）
    中級    （180時間～270時間）
    上級    （270時間以上）

## 学習者の年齢

    6才～8才、6才～10才、6才～13才、
    8才～10才、8才～13才、8才～18才、
    11才～13才、11才～18才、14才～18才
    特になし

## 所要時間

アクティビティにかかる時間のめやす。その場に合わせて、適宜変更してよい。

## あらかじめ必要な知識

アクティビティを行うのにあらかじめ必要な最小限の背景知識や能力。「特になし」とは、それまでのすべての学習事項が含まれる場合である。

## 準備するもの

アクティビティを行うのに必要なもの。ただし、通常、教室に常備されているものは除いている。ほとんど準備の必要がないものから、前もって用意し、あるいは作成しておかなければいけないものまである。いずれにしてもアクティビティの前には何が必要になるか確認しておく必要がある。

## 進め方

アクティビティの手順。

## 先生からのアドバイス

アクティビティを成功させるためのヒントや、アクティビティの応用など、日本語教師の現場の体験から提案である。例えば、年齢の高いクラスで、アクティビティに興味を示さない場合や、日本語に自信がなくてためらっている場合など、学習者にどのようにして興味や自信を持たせ、アクティビティに加われるようにするかなど、実際のクラス運営に役立つアドバイスを行う。

## 付録

巻末の付録。ほとんどのものは、これをコピーすれば、アクティビティの準備ができるように配慮している。また、付録があるものは、原則として本文中にその例が掲載されている。

## 参考文献

Nunan, David. (1988). *The learner-centred Curriculum*. Cambridge: Cambridge University Press.

Nunan, David. (1989). *Designing Tasks for the Communiative Classroom*. Cambridge: Cambridge University Press.

Oxford, Rebecca L. (1990) *Language Learning Strategies: What Every`Teacher Should Know*. Boston, MA: Heinle and Heinle.

\*\*\*

**監修**（以下敬称略・アイウエオ順）
　　上野田鶴子（東京女子大学）
　　岡崎敏雄（筑波大学）
　　西原鈴子（国立国語研究所）

**コーディネート**
カイト由利子（カネディアン・アカデミイ）

**編集**
伊能祥子（セント・メリーズ・インターナショナル・スクール）
植田瑞子（聖心インターナショナルスクール）
太田垣明子（大阪インターナショナルスクール）
清水純子（セント・メリーズ・インターナショナル・スクール）
スコギンズ千枝（サンモール・インターナショナルスクール）
田中小静（アメリカン・スクール・イン・ジャパン）
西原鈴子（国立国語研究所）
林敬子（西町インターナショナルスクール）
ライリー佐知子（セント・ジョセフ・インターナショナル・スクール）

**執筆／執筆協力**
アメリカン・スクール・イン・ジャパン
　　相沢博子・葛西淑子・榛葉久美・田中小静・直井和子・久宗千栄子・松本典子・牛込真紀
大阪インターナショナルスクール
　　大迫奈佳江・太田垣明子・中村亮介

カネディアン・アカデミイ
　　伊藤富美子・大谷藤子・川端由子・妹尾道子・古谷博子・リチェソン久乃

関西　クリスチャン　スクール
　　小林幸子

クリスチャン・アカデミー・イン・ジャパン
　　岩淵順子

サンモール・インターナショナルスクール
　　伊井千鶴子・スコギンズ千枝・早木マユミ・松田順子・百海和子

ジャパン　インターナショナル　スクール
　　大林日美子・妹尾泰子

聖心インターナショナルスクール
　　植田瑞子・川中美早

清泉インターナショナル学園
　　ネイラー市川ますみ

聖ミカエル国際学校
　　赤碕裕美・岡崎政子・牧野田鶴

セント・ジョセフ・インターナショナル・スクール
　　北あゆみ・ライリー佐知子

セント・メリーズ・インターナショナル・スクール
　　伊能祥子・小澤忠助フィリップ・桜井千代子・清水純子・土岐慶子・安成良臣・ユージャック民子

東北インターナショナルスクール
　　宮城京子

西町インターナショナルスクール
　　西町インターナショナルスクールチーム・林敬子

広島国際学園
　　宮城珠子

ブリティッシュスクール　イン　東京
　　平浩子

横浜インターナショナルスクール
　　海野直子・木ノ内和美・竹田眞知子・柳川祐子


イラストレーション協力
トム・ロバーツ（カネディアン・アカデミイ）

本書を刊行するにあたり、次の方々に深く感謝の意を表します。

牛島通彦（財団法人　国際文化フォーラム）、ジェイムズ・ウィージー（元大阪インターナショナルスクール）、鎌田修（京都外国語大学）、財団法人　石橋財団、ミッシェル・ジュトラ（セント・メリーズ・インターナショナル・スクール）、鈴木重好（講談社インターナショナル）、中野佳代子（財団法人　国際文化フォーラム）、日本インターナショナル協議会（JCIS）学校校長および日本語の先生方、日本語プロジェクト運営委員会、福田浩子（湘北短期大学）、マイケル・ブレイズ（講談社インターナショナル）、スー・ヘイル（アメリカン・スクール・イン・ジャパン）、牧野成一（プリンストン大学）、モーサー敦子（カネディアン・アカデミイ）、米山啓子（カネディアン・アカデミイ）

# BITS and PIECES

**51 Activities
for Teaching Japanese
K–12**

# **1** DECODING WORDS

■ **Level of Japanese:** Beginners (basic)

■ **Students' age:** 6 to 8

■ **Required time:** 5 minutes

## AIMS OF THE ACTIVITY

Relating sounds to letters and by extension to the meaning of vocabulary

**Important expressions:**

● None

**What the students must already know:**

● Nothing in particular

**Materials to prepare:**

● A list of words the students have already learned, written incorrectly (i.e., with the syllables in the wrong order)

Example: ごりん = りんご

**Procedure:**

1. The teacher writes a word on the blackboard or on a sheet of paper, with the word's syllables in the wrong order.
2. The students correct the mistakes, putting the syllables in the right order.

**Advice for the teacher:**

● Students learn that Japanese script takes the syllable as the smallest unit of sound.

● This activity can be used as a warming-up exercise at the beginning of class.

## ② WHAT COLOR ARE THE CARDS?

■**Level of Japanese:** Beginners
(basic)

■**Students' age:** 8 to 13

■**Required time:** 5 to 10 minutes

### AIMS OF THE ACTIVITY

Practicing expressions of color

**Important expressions:**

● Words expressing color

E.g., adjectives ending in 一い, such as 赤い and 白い, or modifiers using の, as with 緑の or むらさきの.

**What the students must already know:**

● Words expressing colors

● Names of various things

**Materials to prepare:**

● Square-shaped pieces of thick card in the center of which has been stuck origami paper of varying colors (= the A cards).

● Square-shaped pieces of thick card, each showing the silhouette of a different object (= the B cards): e.g., umbrella, shoe, futon.

**A card**  **B card**

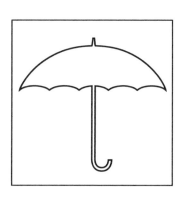

あかい〜
けれしの〜.
ふるい〜
おもい〜.
きのうかった〜
むかえもらった〜

application
picture cards given/shown.
appropriate adjective to add.
so ~~it~~ as many as one
can think
later/could be m~~~~sentences

**Procedure:**

1. Using the A cards, learn or review the names of the colors.

2. Using the B cards, learn or review the names of things.

3. Putting a B card on top of an A card, practice saying 赤いかさ (a red umbrella), 緑のかさ (a green umbrella), etc.

**Advice for the teacher:**

- As students get used to the game, they will be able to quickly put the B cards on the A cards one after another, and go through the colors.

- This can also work well at the start of class as a warming-up activity.

- It is a good idea to keep a stock of pictures of things being studied in class (just trace the shapes and stick them on cards).

**Appendix:**

- Examples of B cards for photocopying.

# **3** THE FISHING GAME

■ **Level of Japanese:** Beginners (basic)

■ **Students' age:** 6 to 8

■ **Required time:** 15 minutes

## AIMS OF THE ACTIVITY

Practicing listening and understanding words

**Important expressions:**

● None

**What the students must already know:**

● The vocabulary studied so far

**Materials to prepare:**

● 10 cm square cards with paperclips attached (10 cards for each group of 5 to 6 students). On the front of the cards there is a picture of a word you have studied. On the back of the cards there is a number indicating how many points are awarded for a correct answer (between 1 and 5).

● Each group needs a fishing pole with a U-shaped magnet hanging from its line.

**Procedure:**

1. Split the class into groups of 5 or 6. Give each group about 10 cards and a fishing pole.
2. Each group forms a circle and puts its cards face-up in the middle.
3. Students use their fishing poles and magnets to pick up the card showing the picture of the word read by the teacher.
4. The group that is quickest to pick up the card gets the number of points written on the back of the card.
5. Group members take turns using the fishing pole.
6. At the end of the round the group with the most points is the winner.

**Advice for the teacher:**

● Young learners are apt to get carried away with the "fishing" part of this activity, so make sure they are actually learning some Japanese as well!

● If the fishing lines get tangled, it can take a long time to get the game going, so make sure the lines are no more than 50 cm long.

● It requires a fair degree of concentration to choose the correct card and "reel it in," so attach light paperclips to the cards which can be easily picked up using the magnets.

# **4** MAKING WORD GROUPS

■ **Level of Japanese:** Beginners

■ **Students' age:** all

■ **Required time:** about 10 minutes for each category

## AIMS OF THE ACTIVITY

Reviewing vocabulary by dividing into categories
words the students have already learned

**Important expressions:**

● None

**What the students must already know:**

● How to read and write hiragana and katakana

**Materials to prepare:**

● One piece of paper for each group

**Procedure:**

1. Divide the class into groups of 2 to 4 students, make sure everyone has a pencil, and have each group sit in a circle.
2. The teacher places a piece of paper in the middle of each group's circle.
3. The teacher gives the class a category.
   Examples: 食べ物、教室にあるもの、動物、カタカナ言葉、赤いもの (food, things to be found in the classroom, animals, words written in katakana, things that are red).
4. The students must write as many words as they can think of that fit the given category or at least have some link with it. They only have a limited amount of time, so must work against the clock. Group members must work together to ensure they do not write the same word twice.
5. When the teacher gives the signal to stop, students put down their pencils.
6. The group that has written the most words is the winner.

**Advice for the teacher:**

● Limit the amount of time for each category, and be careful not to run overtime.

● You might have each group read in front of the class the words it came up with.

● For classes of very young learners you might also use objects or pictures. For example, you might place a ball, a hat, a tomato and other objects, or perhaps models and pictures, around the classroom, and ask the students to collect any round objects they can find. However, the number of students moving around at any one time should be restricted; otherwise the class can end in chaos!

● When using objects or pictures, you might also practice the asking and answering of questions such as: これは何ですか ("What is this?"), トマトです ("It is a tomato").

# **5** MATCHING UP THE CARDS

■ **Level of Japanese:** Beginners

■ **Students' age:** all

■ **Required time:** 10 minutes

## AIMS OF THE ACTIVITY

Practicing words and relating them to their meaning

**Important expressions:**

● だれの番ですか（Whose turn is it?)

● わたしの／あなたの／〜 (student's name) さんの番です　(It is my [my/your/so-and-so's] turn.)

**What the students must already know:**

● How to read the hiragana, katakana, or kanji used in the activity

**Materials to prepare:**

● Picture cards of words the students are studying

● Letter cards with hiragana, katakana, and kanji

● Joker cards

**Procedure:**

1. Divide the class into groups of 5 to 8.

2. Each group sits on the floor in a circle.

3. Shuffle the letter cards and the picture cards together, and deal them out to the class.

4. Decide who is to go first in each group. The player to go first takes one card from the person next to them. If they have a picture card with a matching letter card, they put the matching cards onto the floor in the middle of the group.

5. The second player then takes a card from the next player.

6. The winner of the game is the person who gets rid of his cards first. The person left holding the joker is the loser.

**Advice for the teacher:**

● If you are not good at drawing pictures, you can cut out photographs and illustrations from books to make the picture cards.

● If there are too many cards, the game can go on forever. For a group of 5 students 30 cards or less is about right.

 **WIN AT CARDS!**

■ **Level of Japanese:** Beginners

■ **Students' age:** 6 to 10

■ **Required time:** 5 to 20 minutes

## AIMS OF THE ACTIVITY

### Reading and pronunciation

**Important expressions:**

• None

**What the students must already know:**

• How to read the hiragana, katakana, or kanji used in the activity

**Materials to prepare:**

• Cards the size of playing cards. For example:

46 hiragana cards
Verb cards (with verbs in hiragana on the front, and pictures on the back)
Adjective cards (with adjectives in hiragana on the front, and pictures on the back)
Noun cards (with hiragana on the front, and pictures on the back)

## Procedure:

1. Students find a partner and form a pair.

2. Students shuffle the cards and take turns showing their partner one card at a time.

3. Students first show the front (text side) of the card and see if their partner can correctly read it.

4. After going through the stack once, students reshuffle the cards and show the back of the card to see if their partner can guess the correct word that describes the picture.

## Advice for the teacher:

- Students can also use the cards to study on their own.

- You can make this into a game, with the student in each pair who can read the most cards in a given time (or the one who can correctly read the most cards out of a given number) being the winner. The teacher or a student may act as referee.

- You can also make it into a tournament involving the whole class, with each pair acting as a team.

- You can also have students repeat over and over any cards they get wrong.

**7** **PLEASE GO STRAIGHT**

■ **Level of Japanese:** Beginners

■ **Students' age:** all

■ **Required time:** 15 minutes

## AIMS OF THE ACTIVITY

Acting out the meaning of words and sentences using the body

**Important expressions:**

- まっすぐ行ってください (Please go straight.)
- 右に曲がってください (Please turn right.)
- 左に曲がってください (Please turn left.)
- 止まってください (Please stop.)

**What the students must already know:**

- Expressions of place （ここ、そこ、右、左、かど、信号、つきあたり、〜を、〜まで）
- Expressions of movement （行ってください、曲がってください、止まってください）

**Materials to prepare:**

- Something to cover the eyes (such as an eye mask or a towel)
- Move the desks to make roads or pathways in the classroom

**Procedure:**

1. The whole class learns expressions for asking directions.
2. In pairs, student A covers his/her eyes while student B stands behind him/her.
3. Student B gives student A directions, and together they make their way from the starting line to the finish line.

**Advice for the teacher:**

- Increase the number of directions as the students' Japanese improves.
- If it is difficult to move around in the classroom due to a lack of space, you can use a picture of a town (with roads, traffic lights, buildings, parks, etc.), with a building block, coin, etc. serving as a person, moving it around the picture. See appendix.
- Point out that many streets and roads in Japan do not have names. As a result, general expressions along the lines of "Turn right at the corner" （かどを右に曲がってください） are often used when giving directions.

**Appendix:**

- Map

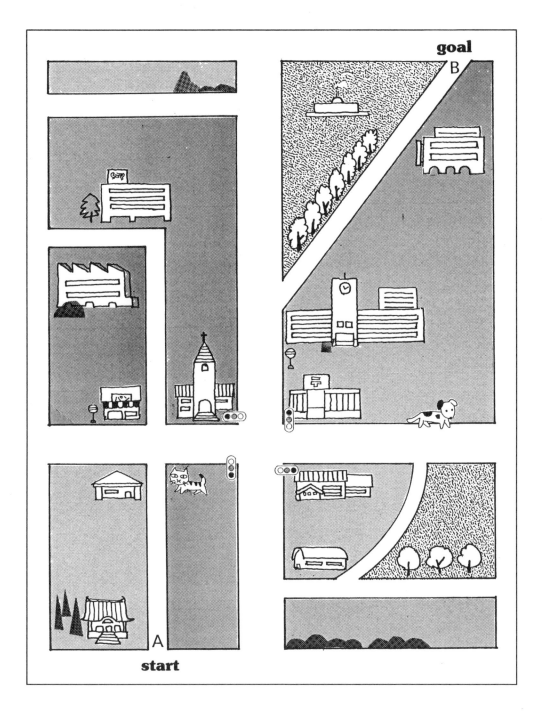

**References:**

- *Iki Iki Nihongo*. Kazue Fukuda, Contee Seely, Elizabeth Romijin, Mary S. Noguchi. Berkeley, CA: Command Performance Language Institute, 1994.

# ❽ WHAT'S IN THE BOX?

- **Level of Japanese:** Beginners
- **Students' age:** 6 to 8
- **Required time:** 5 minutes

## AIMS OF THE ACTIVITY

### Listening carefully to words

**Important expressions:**

- 箱の中にあるものは何ですか （What's in the box?）
- 赤いものです。着るものです （It's something red. It's something you wear.）
- 〜です （It's ~.）

**What the students must already know:**

- The vocabulary studied so far

**Materials to prepare:**

- A small box or can with a large question mark written on the front.
- Put between one and five cards into the box (or can). On the cards are pictures representing letters, words, or phrases that have been previously studied.

  For example:

**Procedure:**

1. Students take turns guessing what pictures (letters or words) are in the box. The teacher decides the range of vocabulary to be covered (e.g., from the previous lesson or something more extensive).
2. Students should listen carefully to what others answer so as not to repeat them.
3. When a student guesses correctly, the card is removed from the box.

**Advice for the teacher:**

- Use this activity in the first or the last five minutes of class.

- Ask students quickly one after another in seating order, and if any spend too long thinking, go straight to the next.

- If no one has got a right answer after everyone has had a try, give the class some hints: e.g., 着る もの、食べ物、赤いもの

- Emphasize that students should remember what has already been guessed.

- To ensure that some students do not dominate the activity, ask the students in turn, making sure they all have an equal chance to answer.

| **9** | THE NUMBERS GAME | ■ Level of Japanese: Beginners |
|---|---|---|
| | | ■ Students' age: 6 to 13 |
| | | ■ Required time: 10 minutes |

### AIMS OF THE ACTIVITY

Using physical response or sensation / Having fun learning numbers
using the whole body / Improving coordination

**Important expressions:**

● Cardinal numbers

いち、に、さん、し（よん）、ご、ろく、しち（なな）、はち、く（きゅう）、じゅう、じゅういち、じゅうに、じゅうさん、じゅうし（じゅうよん）、じゅうご、じゅうろく、じゅうしち（じゅうなな）、じゅうはち、じゅうく（じゅうきゅう）、にじゅう

**What the students must already know:**

● How to count up to at least twenty

**Materials to prepare:**

● None

**Procedure:**

1. Make groups of 5 to 10 students, each group sitting in a circle.

2. In consecutive order, give each student a number.

3. Tell all the students in a group to do the following (to a 4-4 rhythm):

   On the first beat: hit your knees with your hands

   On the second beat: clap your hands

   On the third beat: snap the thumb and middle finger of your right hand

   On the fourth beat: snap the thumb and middle finger of your left hand

4. On the third beat, the student to start says his (her) number, and then on the fourth beat says at random any of the numbers that have been assigned.

5. The student whose number matches that given at random then repeats step #4.

**Advice for the teacher:**

● If the class has only just learned how to say numbers in Japanese, it is a good idea to write the numbers down on cards and put them where the students can see them.

● To say the numbers while clapping hands etc. requires a fair degree of coordination, so proceed at a speed that is suitable for the students' age and ability.

● This can also be used to practice saying numbers that sound similar (e.g., し and しち).

# ⑩ LET'S MAKE FRIENDS

■ **Level of Japanese:** Beginners

■ **Students' age:** 6 to 10

■ **Required time:** 10 minutes

## AIMS OF THE ACTIVITY

Practicing listening to and understanding words

**Important expressions:**

● ～ですか （Is it ~?）
はい、そうです （Yes, it is.）
いいえ、ちがいます （No, it isn't.）

● ～を持っていますか （Do you have a ~?）
はい、持っています （Yes, I do.）
いいえ、持っていません （No, I don't.）

**What the students must already know:**

● Words for numbers, colors, animals, shapes

**Materials to prepare:**

● The same number of types of picture card as there are groups, and the same number of cards as there are people playing the game (e.g., if there are 5 groups of 3 people, you will need 5 types of cards and 3 of each to form one set)

● A bag containing one set of picture cards for each group

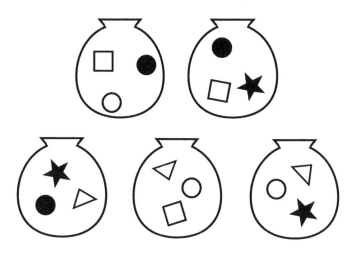

**Procedure:**

1. Form the number of groups appropriate to the size of the class; each group with the same number of students.

2. Give each group a bag of cards.

3. Each player takes one card from the bag, and without showing it to the other players holds it against their chest.

4. At a sign from the teacher all the students stand up and walk around the classroom asking other students what card they hold. The questions and answers should take one of the following forms:

Questions: 赤い丸ですか。
赤い丸を持っていますか。

Answers: はい、そうです。
いいえ、違います。
持っています。
いいえ、持っていません。

5. When a student finds someone with the same card, they both sit down.

**Advice for the teacher:**

- The teacher walks around checking that the students are not showing each other their picture cards but using the questions and answers shown above.

- Instead of using picture cards you might try using small toys such as plastic fruit and vegetables or rubber animals (used as erasers). However, it is worth bearing in mind that collecting them (getting them all back) after the activity is over can be difficult.

- The questions and answers given above are not the only ones that can be used. Students may be more colloquial. For example:

持って(い)る？
うん、持って(い)る。
ううん、持って(い)ない。

# **11** WHAT TIME IS IT?

- ■ **Level of Japanese:** Beginners
- ■ **Students' age:** 8 to 18
- ■ **Required time:** 20 minutes

## AIMS OF THE ACTIVITY

Practicing naturally / Using expressions of time

**Important expressions:**

- もしもし。そちらでは、今何時ですか (Hello, what time is it there?)
- 〜では、〜時です (In ~ it is ~ o'clock.)
- Names of principal capital cities around the world in Japanese.
- 朝、昼、夕方、夜中、晩

**What the students must already know:**

- How to ask and answer simple questions

**Materials to prepare:**

- A toy telephone
- A world map showing the different time zones (see appendix)

**Procedure:**

1. Two students (A and B) form a pair and do a role-play. Decide with the students what roles they will act out. They might want to be a foreign correspondent and a local journalist working for a newspaper, or two members of a family, or perhaps even an international telephone operator and a customer.

2. もしもし。こちらAです。今〜 (name of capital city) では〜時ですが、そちらでは今何時ですか。
   こちらはBです。〜 (name of capital city) では、〜時ですよ。

**Advice for the teacher:**

- You might also wish to teach the students useful expressions of apology when making telephone calls early in the morning and late at night (朝早く／夜遅くすみません).

**Appendix:**

- A world map showing the different time zones

**(12)** THE ASSOCIATION GAME

■ **Level of Japanese:** Beginners

■ **Students' age:** 6 to 13

■ **Required time:** 15 minutes

## AIMS OF THE ACTIVITY

Practicing words and relating them to their meanings

**Important expressions:**

● None

**What the students must already know:**

● Nothing in particular

**Materials to prepare:**

● A list of words learned so far and some hints to help students remember them

**Procedure:**

1. Divide the class into groups.

2. The teacher chooses a word and gives the class a hint to help them guess what the word is.

3. The groups listen to the teacher's hint and take turns in guessing what the word is.

4. If after one round, none of the groups gets the right answer, the teacher gives another hint and starts over. For example, if the problem word is (お)箸, or chopsticks, the exchange might go as follows:

    Teacher:  ヒント1。「長い」です
    Group A:  へび
    Group B:  ロープ
    Teacher:  ヒント2。「食べる」です
    Group A:  にんじん
    Group B:  (お)そば
    Teacher:  ヒント3。「2本」です
    Group A:  (お)はし
    Teacher:  あたり！グループAの勝ち。

5. The winning group starts the next round.

**Advice for the teacher:**

● Depending on the students' level of Japanese, you may wish to give the hints in English (or their mother tongue).

● Think of your hints beforehand, and give them one after another at a quickish tempo.

● To make sure the activity moves along speedily, you may want to limit the time each group has for making their guess (using a bell to signal when their time is up).

● Having one of the students read out the hints can work well, but this tends to slow the activity down.

# 13 PUT IN THE RIGHT A, I, U, E, O ORDER

■ **Level of Japanese:** Beginners

■ **Students' age:** 6 to 13

■ **Required time:** 20 minutes

## AIMS OF THE ACTIVITY

Learning the phonetic alphabet and words expressing spatial relations

**Important expressions:**

● となり（上、下、前、後ろ、つぎ）は何ですか (What is beside [above, below, before, behind, following] it?)

**What the students must already know:**

● How to read hiragana
● How to ask and answer simple questions

**Materials to prepare:**

● One set of hiragana and katakana cards for each group (each card shows one kana of the 50 in the kana alphabet)

**Procedure:**

1. Divide the class into groups of 5 or 6.
2. Each group sits in a circle, with enough space in the center so that the 50 kana cards can be spread out in *a, i, u, e, o* order.
3. A set of cards is given to each group. The cards are shuffled and put in one place, face down.
4. The groups decide who is to go first (using paper, scissors or stone). The first person takes one card from the pack and puts it in the center of the circle.
5. The second person to go (either chosen by doing paper, scissors or stone again, or by going clockwise around the circle) takes a card; if the card shows a kana which comes next (in *a, i, u, e, o* order) to one of those already on the floor, the card may be put down. If not, the card must be kept, and the player says "pass." Then the next person takes a card. The game is over when all 50 cards have been put down in the correct order.
6. Players may either put down one of the cards they picked up earlier and kept, or they may take another card from the pack.
7. A player may pass only three times. At the fourth pass, the player is out, and must put down all his or her cards in the correct alphabetical place.
8. The winner is the person who gets rid of their cards the quickest.

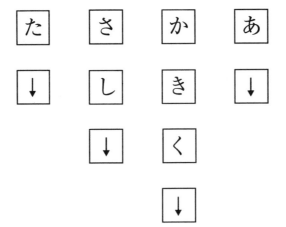

**Advice for the teacher:**

- Write the kana on the cards as large as possible so they are easy to read.

- Knowing the Japanese *a, i, u, e, o* alphabetical order is useful when using a dictionary and learning the conjugation of verbs.

- If you make cards with particles and verbs written on them, you can also make short sentences, and use them for other games.

# 14 HIRAGANA SCRABBLE

■ **Level of Japanese:** Beginners

■ **Students' age:** all

■ **Required time:** 15 to 20 minutes

## AIMS OF THE ACTIVITY

Practicing words and relating them to their meanings

**Important expressions:**

- ちょっと待ってください (Please wait a moment.)
- 次は、だれの番ですか (Whose turn is it next?)

**What the students must already know:**

- How to read and write hiragana and katakana

**Materials to prepare:**

- A scrabble board (a large piece of paper will do) with the first word already written by the teacher. The board should be at least 9 squares by 9 squares in size. (See appendix.) Examples of the first word to be written by the teacher:

  げつようび
  さくら
  おはよう
  ありがとう

**Procedure:**

1. Divide the class into groups of 2 or 3 students.
2. Give each group a scrabble board with one word already written in the center.
3. Taking turns, the students use the letters on the board to make new words, writing them vertically from top to bottom or horizontally from left to right on the board. Thus, if the word supplied by the teacher is ありがとう, the students could use the letters ご and ん and add them to り to produce りんご.

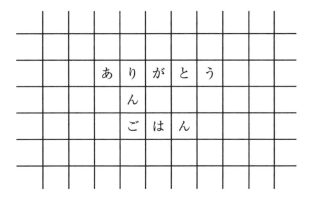

**Advice for the teacher:**

- Make sure the class does not write from bottom to top or from right to left.

- If you want to do this activity as a class and not in groups, use an overhead projector (or the blackboard).

**Appendix:**

- Scrabble board

## 15 THE WAY I AM

■ **Level of Japanese:** Beginners

■ **Students' age:** 6 to 13

■ **Required time:** 2 to 3 minutes

### AIMS OF THE ACTIVITY

Practicing with words and relating them to their meanings

**Important expressions:**

● わたしの顔には、穴が7つ (I have seven holes in my head.)

**What the students must already know:**

● The names of parts of the body

**Materials to prepare:**

● None

**Procedure:**

1. Students chant the following verse while pointing with their fingers, stretching out their arms and legs, or clapping their hands.

| = ♩   ↑ = ♪

◻ = ♫   z = 𝄽

わたしの 顔には、 穴が ななつ、

Form a circle and all stand straight. Alternatively, the teacher stands at the front and faces the class. At a signal from the teacher, the students begin chanting the verse.

めに　　　ひと一つ　ふたつ

(As the students say ひと一つ　ふたつ, they point first at one eye and then the other with the index finger.)

はなに　　ひと一つ　ふたつ

(As they say ひと一つ　ふたつ, they point first at one nostril and then the other.)

みみに　　ひと一つ　ふたつ

(As they say ひと一つ　ふたつ, they point first at one ear and then the other.)

23

くちに　　　ひとーつ

（As they say ひとーつ, they point to their mouth.）

わたしの　　てあしは　　よんほん

（Standing up straight.）

てが　　　　いっぽん　　にーほん

（Stretching one arm after another up and out towards the ceiling.）

あしが　　　いっぽん　　にーほん

（Stretching one leg after another out toward the side.）

（During this rest, the students do a little jump into the air and put their arms and legs back at their sides as they were at the start. Then stand up straight.）

わたしの　　まわりに　　は

まえと　　うしろ

（Saying the と of まえと, they clap their hands in front. When saying the ろ of うしろ, they clap their hands behind their back.）

うえと　　した

（Stretching their arms up over their heads, they clap their hands when they say the と of うえと. Bringing their arms down low, they clap their hands again after saying した.）

みぎと　　ひだり

（On the と of みぎと, they put their hands to the right and clap. On the り of ひだり, they put them to their left and clap again.）

ひとーつ　　ふたつ　　　みっつ　　　よっつ

♪ | ♪　　　⊓ |　　　 | |　　　 | |

いつつ　　　むっつ　　　ぜんぶで　　むっつ

⊓ |　　　 | |　　　 ⊓ ⊓　　　 | |

(Students clap their hands in the order given above: i.e., in front, behind their backs, above their heads, then down again, to the right and then to the left, then on ぜんぶで they whirl their arms around in big circles, and on the final syllable of むっつ they clap their hands in front of their chests.)

**Advice for the teacher:**

- This activity can be done in a short time so it can be used effectively as a warming-up exercise at the beginning of each class. As the students move their bodies in time to the verse, they can enjoy themselves as though singing a song.

- In this activity no vocabulary or grammar is taught, but the students get used to the rhythm of Japanese through sound and gesture, so when you do come to introduce a new point of grammar or vocabulary, you will find that everything goes smoothly.

- If you think the verse is too long to do all at one time, practice the part わたしの顔には several times to get used to it, then do the わたしのてあし part. Later add on the わたしのまわりには part, and finally the ひとつ、ふたつ finale!

**16** CONCENTRATION

- **Level of Japanese:** Beginners
- **Students' age:** all
- **Required time:** 10 to 15 minutes

### AIMS OF THE ACTIVITY

Practicing with words and relating them to their meanings

**Important expressions:**

• None

**What the students must already know:**

• How to read hiragana and katakana

**Materials to prepare:**

• 2 sets of about 15 cards, one set showing words written in hiragana, and the other showing the same words written in katakana

**Procedure:**

1. Divide the class into groups of 5 or 6.
2. Shuffle the two sets of cards and lay them out on a table face down.
3. Decide who will go first (using paper, scissors or stone).
4. Turn one card over and read aloud the word written on it. If the player cannot read the card, it is put back face down again; if able to read it correctly, the player turns over another card.
5. If the second card matches the first, the player gets to keep both cards. If not, the cards are returned face down onto the table.
6. The person with the most cards at the end of the game is the winner.

**Advice for the teacher:**

• Depending on the students' level of Japanese, it is a good idea to make sets of picture cards and kanji cards as well, and use different combinations of sets to add variety to the activity (for example, you might try using picture cards with hiragana cards, or hiragana cards with kanji cards).

• Instead of having the students simply read the cards aloud, it can be more fun to get them guessing and using their minds. For example, if the cards りんご and さくら are turned over, the student answers 食べ物です.

• If you laminate the cards, they will last a long time. It can also be fun to have the students draw the pictures to be used on the picture cards.

**17 GESTURES**

■ **Level of Japanese:** Beginners

■ **Students' age:** 11 to 13

■ **Required time:** 15 to 20 minutes

## AIMS OF THE ACTIVITY

Expressing the meaning of words and phrases using the body

**Important expressions:**

- わたしはだれでしょう （Who am I?）
- わたしは何でしょう （What am I?）
- 何をしていますか （What are you doing?）
   ～をしています （I'm doing ~.）

**What the students must already know:**

- How to write simple sentences

**Materials to prepare:**

- Cards with one word written on them (each team to be given 6 cards)

**Procedure:**

1. Students divide up into two teams of 3 to 6 students.
2. One person from each team looks at a card and checks its meaning with the teacher, making sure none of the other students can hear what is said.
3. Within a given time the student must convey the meaning of the word on the card to the team members through the use of gestures.
4. If the team guesses the right answer, they get a point. If they get it wrong, the other team gets a chance to answer.

**Advice for the teacher:**

- The words, phrases, or sentences written on the cards to be acted out in gestures should be appropriate to the students' level of Japanese. If using words, you might want to divide them into categories (such as family, animals, or occupations), and let students know which category the word being mimed is taken from.
- With large classes you can have pairs of teams compete at the same time. If space is limited, do the activity with just two teams and have the rest of the class watch the contest.

## 18 PRACTICING なる (TO BECOME)

- **Level of Japanese:** Beginners (basic, intermediate)
- **Students' age:** all
- **Required time:** 10 minutes

### AIMS OF THE ACTIVITY

Learning to use *-i* adjectives and *-na* adjectives,
and combining them with the verb なる

**Important expressions:**

- ～になりました（It has gotten ~.)
- ～くなりました（It has gotten ~.)

**What the students must already know:**

- *-i* adjectives and *-na* adjectives
- The present and past tenses of verbs

**Materials to prepare:**

- One large piece of paper (anything will do as long as it is large enough for the whole class to see)

**Procedure:**

1. Show the class one piece of paper, and say これは紙です。1枚です.
2. Cut the paper in half, and say 2枚になりました.
3. Cut each piece of paper into halves, and say 4枚になりました.
4. Cutting the paper into ever smaller pieces, say 小さくなりました.
5. After the paper is in tiny pieces, crumple it up and say ゴミになりました.
6. Throw the rubbish (onto the desk) and say きたなくなりました.
7. Pick up the rubbish and say きれいになりました.

**Advice for the teacher:**

- This activity can be used as a way of introducing or going over *-i* adjectives and *-na* adjectives.
- Draw attention to the fact that きれいな and 有名な are *-na* adjectives.
- Instead of the teacher saying all the things listed above in steps 1 to 7, let the students go in halfway and say some of them.

# 19 LET'S GO FOR A WALK

■ **Level of Japanese:** Beginners
　　　　　　　　　　　(basic, intermediate)
■ **Students' age:** all

■ **Required time:** 45 to 60 minutes

## AIMS OF THE ACTIVITY

Practicing words and relating them to their meanings

**Important expressions:**

• None

**What the students must already know:**

• How to read and write hiragana and katakana

**Materials to prepare:**

• Permission from the school to take students on an excursion

• Paper for making notes

• A hard folder to be used as a writing table

• A pencil

**Procedure:**

1. Decide on a route to be walked by the teacher and the students.
2. Decide what things are to be looked for when out on the walk.
   (E.g.: words written in katakana, things that move, round objects, etc.)
3. Divide the class into groups of 2 or 3.
4. Go out for a walk.
5. Each group writes down and makes a note of what it finds.
6. Each group tells the class, or puts up for viewing, what words it wrote down.

**Advice for the teacher:**

• For those living outside of Japan, the students can be taken to nearby Japanese restaurants or supermarkets.

• It is a good idea to invite the students' parents along.

• You can also have the class look for 50 words all beginning with a different kana of the Japanese alphabet. It is a good way of teaching the class that no words begin with the letter ん! (See appendix.)

**Appendix:**

• A sheet to be used when looking for words that begin with the different kana of the Japanese alphabet

**20** **DO THEY SELL IT OR NOT?**

- **Level of Japanese:** Beginners (basic, intermediate)
- **Students' age:** all
- **Required time:** 15 to 45 minutes

### AIMS OF THE ACTIVITY

Practicing the *-te* form

**Important expressions:**

- 売って（い）ますか (Do they sell it?)
- はい、売って（い）ます (Yes, they do.)
- いいえ、売って（い）ません (No, they don't.)

**What the students must already know:**

- How to ask and answer simple questions
- Aural comprehension of simple sentences

**Materials to prepare:**

- Worksheets for the questions (see appendix; example below)

| 店の名前 ＼ 品名 | フィルム | カメラ | ボールペン |
|---|---|---|---|
| ABCマート | | | |
| XYZマート | | | |
| 123ショップ | | | |

**Procedure:**

1. Write on the worksheet the name of a local store that everyone knows.

2. The teacher asks the class whether that store sells a certain product; if the answer is positive, the students write an O, and if it is negative, they write an X on their worksheet.

   Q: ～で～を売っていますか。

   A: はい、売っています。

   いいえ、売っていません。

3. Divide the class into groups of 4 or 5 students.

4. Based on the completed worksheet, students take turns asking and answering questions about the stores and products.

**Advice for the teacher:**

- This activity is also an effective way of enlarging the students' everyday vocabulary.

- Each group can decide the names of stores and specific products, and prepare their own worksheets. Each group can report the results to the class after completing the activity.

**Appendix:**

- Worksheet

**21** **WHAT'S IN THE BAG?**

- ■ **Level of Japanese:** Beginners (basic, intermediate)
- ■ **Students' age:** all
- ■ **Required time:** 15 to 20 minutes

## AIMS OF THE ACTIVITY

## Practicing words

**Important expressions:**

- 〜らしい (It seems to be ~.)

**What the students must already know:**

- Nouns / verbs (in the dictionary form) ＋ らしい

**Materials to prepare:**

- Bags (preferably made of cloth or some material that can be easily tied)
- Things to put in the bags (erasers, dice, sponges, tennis balls, paper cups, etc., enough for all the players)

**Procedure:**

1. Divide the class into groups of 4 or 5. Give each group a bag with some items inside.
2. One by one the students put their hand into the bag and say 〜(が入っている)らしい. They can only hazard a guess at what it is they are feeling, so if they are wrong, it does not matter. Each player should remember what they have touched.
3. The group members pool their information, make guesses as to all of the items in the bag, and write down their ideas.
4. Each group tells the class what they have written.
5. Finally the bags are emptied and everyone sees what was really in them!

**Advice for the teacher:**

- It is a good idea to put things of a similar size, weight, and feel into the bags.
- You can also use this activity to teach the class the usage of *na* adjectives ＋ らしい. That is, there is no *na* between the *na* adjective and らしい: e.g., きれいらしい.
- You might want to give a small prize (such as some decals) to the team that guesses all the objects in the bag correctly.

## 22 TO HAVE OR HAVE NOT

■ **Level of Japanese:** Beginners
(basic, intermediate)
■ **Students' age:** all

■ **Required time:** 15 minutes

### AIMS OF THE ACTIVITY

Practicing the *-te* form

**Important expressions:**

● 〜(を)持っていますか (Do you have a ~?)
● はい、持っています (Yes, I do.)
● いいえ、持っていません (No, I don't.)

**What the students must already know:**

● Asking and answering simple questions
● Aural comprehension of simple sentences

**Materials to prepare:**

● Worksheets (see example below)

| 名前 ＼ 品名 | ファミコン | ビデオ | 千円札 |
|---|---|---|---|
| ローラ | | | |
| トム | | | |
| ジョニー | | | |

**Procedure:**

1. At first the teacher practices with the whole class as follows.

Question: 〜さん、ファミコンを持っていますか。
(_____, do you have a video game player?)

Answer: はい、持っています。 (Yes, I do.)
いいえ、持っていません。 (No, I don't.)

2. The teacher asks a question and a student answers. The other students listen and write either an O, meaning "yes," or an X, meaning "no," in the appropriate slots on their worksheet.

3. Then divide the class into groups of at least 3 students (one to ask questions, one to answer, and one to write down the answers) and have them practice.

4. Each group thinks of a set of questions, and asks them using the format described above in (1).

33

5. Finally students summarize the contents of their worksheets and tell the class the results. For example:

～さんは、＿＿＿＿＿を持っています。(＿＿＿＿ has a ＿＿＿＿.)

＿＿＿＿＿は、2人の人が持っています。(Two people have ＿＿＿＿.)

**Advice for the teacher:**

● Explain the difference between あります and 持っています as this can often be a cause of confusion.

● When asking their classmates about what things they have, make sure no one feels their privacy is being invaded. Items that might be asked about include bus or train passes, bank books, money, photos of friends, comic books, and posters.

● In the beginning it is a good idea to limit the number of things being asked about.

**Appendix:**

● Worksheet

# WHAT'S THE ODD ONE OUT?

■ **Level of Japanese:** Beginners (basic, intermediate)

■ **Students' age:** 8 to 10

■ **Required time:** 5 minutes

## AIMS OF THE ACTIVITY

Reviewing the meaning of vocabulary learned so far /
Concentrating on improving listening ability

**Important expressions:**

● よく聞いてください。この中で、違っているのはどれですか。1つ選んでください。

(Listen carefully. Among these things, which doesn't belong? Choose one.)

**What the students must already know:**

● The vocabulary studied so far

**Materials to prepare:**

● From the vocabulary learned so far choose ten groups of four words each; each group should have a common theme with one word being the odd one out. For example:

りんご　いぬ　バナナ　いちご

In this example the answer is いぬ (dog), the other three being kinds of fruit.

**Procedure:**

1. The teacher says to the whole class: よく聞いてください。この中で、違っているのはどれですか。1つ選んでください。

2. The teacher (or a student) reads the four words to the class.

3. The student who guesses which one is the odd one out raises his or her hand and answers the question.

4. The student who answers must also say why it is the odd one out (if they cannot explain this in Japanese, they may use English or their mother tongue).

**Advice for the teacher:**

● Take care over how fast the words are read out. It is preferable to read them at as natural a speed as possible, but it may be necessary to read difficult words a little more slowly.

● To liven up the class it can be fun to include words taken from areas not yet studied in class. For example:

おすし　チャーハン　天ぷら　うどん

● Depending on the level of the students' Japanese, the teacher or a student can pick the odd one out from a group of four items and explain their reasons for choosing it. In the above example the answer given might be うどん, and the reason given might be スープ／汁に入っている から (It is the only one containing a soup or broth).

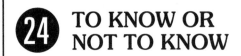

**24** **TO KNOW OR NOT TO KNOW**

■ **Level of Japanese:** Beginners
(basic, intermediate)
■ **Students' age:** all

■ **Required time:** 15 minutes

### AIMS OF THE ACTIVITY

Practicing the *-te* form

**Important expressions:**

● 〜を知っていますか (Do you know _____?)

● はい、知っています (Yes, I do.)

● いいえ、知りません (No, I don't.)

**What the students must already know:**

● Asking and answering simple questions

● Aural comprehension of simple sentences

**Materials to prepare:**

● Questions worksheet. For example:

| 名前　　項目 | 先生の電話番号 | ビルのくつのサイズ | レインさんの住所 |
|---|---|---|---|
| ナオミ | | | |
| デイビッド | | | |
| ポーラ | | | |

**Procedure:**

1. The teacher first practices with the whole class.

2. The teacher selects a student and asks a question. The student replies.

   Question:　先生の電話番号を知っていますか。

   　　　　　　(Do you know the teacher's telephone number?)

   Answer:　はい、知っています。(Yes, I do.)

   　　　　　いいえ、知りません。(No, I don't.)

3. The other students listen to the answer and write either an O, meaning "yes," or an X, meaning "no," on their worksheet.

4. Then divide the class into groups of four or five.

5. A student takes the place of the teacher and asks questions to be answered by the other members of the group (see 2). Students write down the questions and answers on their worksheets.

**Advice for the teacher:**

- Draw students' attention to the negative form (not 知<sub>し</sub>っていません but 知<sub>し</sub>りません).
- Think of fun questions to ask such as Xさん (a celebrity) の誕生日<sub>たんじょうび</sub>はいつなのか知<sub>し</sub>ってい ますか "Do you know when X's birthday is?" or Yさんの趣味<sub>しゅみ</sub>はなんなのか知<sub>し</sub>っています か "Do you know what Y's hobby is?"
- Instead of questions of the type "Do you know + Noun?" you can also have the class ask questions such as Xさんがいつアメリカに行<sub>い</sub>くのか知<sub>し</sub>っていますか (Do you know when X is going to the USA?) or Yさんが何時<sub>なんじ</sub>に起<sub>お</sub>きたか知<sub>し</sub>っていますか (Do you know what time Y got up this morning?).

**Appendix:**

- Worksheet

# ㉕ CROSSWORD PUZZLE

■ **Level of Japanese:** Beginners
(basic, intermediate)

■ **Students' age:** all

■ **Required time:** 20 minutes

## AIMS OF THE ACTIVITY

Analyzing and practicing writing systems /
Practicing relating words to their meanings

**Important expressions:**

• None

**What the students must already know:**

• How to read the words they have previously studied

**Materials to prepare:**

• A crossword puzzle (words in the puzzle should have something in common: family relationships [father, mother, etc.] or kinds of vehicles [car, truck, etc.]).

**Procedure:**

1. Tell the class what is the largest possible number of words that can be found.

2. At the sign to begin, the students start searching for the words hidden in the crossword puzzle, circling those found.

**Advice for the teacher:**

• Depending on the students' level of Japanese, you may want to give them some hints to help them while they are looking. To make it easier for them, you can say the clues in English (or the students' mother tongue). For example: for いぬ, the hint could be "man's best friend."

• If you want to have the students practice their writing skills, you can have them write down the words found in the crossword puzzle on a separate sheet of paper.

• With younger learners who have only just started learning to write Japanese, you may want to write the words on the blackboard.

**Appendix:**

• A crossword puzzle including words that are often used as greetings or responses.

• A crossword puzzle including the names of things commonly found in the classroom.

• A crossword puzzle including the names of the animals of the Chinese calendar (and an accompanying sheet telling you where all the words are).

# 26 ROULETTE

■ **Level of Japanese:** Beginners, (basic, intermediate)
■ **Students' age:** 6 to 10
■ **Required time:** 10 to 15 minutes

## AIMS OF THE ACTIVITY

Learning to connect numbers and words

**Important expressions:**

- Counters (suffixes used when counting differently shaped objects: e.g., 〜こ、〜本、〜枚)
- Connecting numerical and color expressions with nouns

**What the students must already know:**

- Numbers and the names of colors
- How to read kana (and some kanji, depending on the level)

**Materials to prepare:**

- Cards with the names of things (one name on each card); more cards will be needed than the number of students in the class
- 2 roulette wheels (on one you write numbers, on the other colors). See appendix

**Procedure:**

1. Divide the class into groups of 3 or 4.
2. The students form a circle (either sitting in their groups on the floor or sitting around a round table) in the center of which they put the roulette wheels.
3. Put the cards in a pile and have each student take a card.
4. The students decide which group will go first, and they spin the arrows on the roulette wheels.
5. When the arrows stop spinning, the students must combine the number and color pointed to by the arrows together with the word on the card.

   Example:

   1＋しろい＋ ほん ／3＋あかい＋ えんぴつ

6. The students use the correct counter for the object and say the phrase. For example:
   1さつの白い本, 3本の赤いえんぴつ
      or
   白い本1さつ、赤いえんぴつ3本

**Advice for the teacher:**

- The teacher can make the roulette wheels or have the students make them.
- Depending on the level of the students' Japanese, you might want to add a few simple kanji expressions (to write on the cards).

**Appendix:**

- Roulette wheels

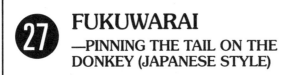

# 27 FUKUWARAI
—PINNING THE TAIL ON THE DONKEY (JAPANESE STYLE)

■ **Level of Japanese:** Beginners (basic, intermediate)

■ **Students' age:** all

■ **Required time:** 10 to 15 minutes

## AIMS OF THE ACTIVITY

Having fun learning the names of parts of the body

**Important expressions:**

- もっと右（左、上、下）へ (More to the right, more to the left, higher, lower)
- 目、耳、鼻、口、まゆ

**What the students must already know:**

- Nothing in particular

**Materials to prepare:**

- Pictures of faces with no eyes, nose and mouth; pictures of eyes, pictures of noses, and pictures of mouths (see appendix)
- Something to cover the eyes

**Procedure:**

1. Divide the class into groups of 4 or 5.
2. The students decide who will go first (using paper, scissors or stone).
3. The player covers the eyes so he/she cannot see. Thus blindfolded, the player takes a picture of the eyes, the nose, or the mouth, and tries to place it on the blank face.
4. The other people in the group help them by saying もっと右へ etc.

**Advice for the teacher:**

- Depending on the age of the class, it might be fun to make picture portraits of celebrities and characters from stories to be used in this activity.
- You can also use cartoons taken from newspapers and magazines and enlarge them on a photocopier.
- If using the pictures in the appendix, you might want to explain some of the cultural background and customs concerning *fukuwarai*, *okame* and *hyottoko*.

**Appendix:**

- Two examples of *fukuwarai* (*okame* and *hyottoko*)

| **28** | **THE ICE-CREAM SHOP** | ■ **Level of Japanese:** Beginners (intermediate, advanced)<br>■ **Students' age:** 6 to 10<br><br>■ **Required time:** 30 minutes |

### AIMS OF THE ACTIVITY

Learning how to use words and expressions suitable for a given situation

**Important expressions:**

- これは何ですか (What is this?)
- バニラ／チョコレート／ストロベリーです (It's vanilla, [chocolate, strawberry].)
- コーンですか、カップですか (A cone or a cup?)
- シングルですか、ダブルですか (A single scoop or a double?)
- ～（つ）ください (I'll have ~ [a number].)
- いくらですか (How much is it?)

**What the students must already know:**

- Expressions needed when going shopping

**Materials to prepare:**

- An ice-cream vendor's hat
- Pictures of ice-cream cones or cups; or fan-shaped paper to make the cones and square paper to make the cups; and three types of thin colored paper to roll into a ball and place on cones or in cups to represent ice cream of different flavors.
- Toy money (Japanese yen)

**Procedure:**

1. The whole class practices saying expressions needed when buying ice cream (e.g., the names of flavors, prices, etc.).

2. Making ice-cream cones and cups:

   Cones: Roll fan-shaped paper (as seen in the illustration) into the shape of a cone, gluing or taping the edges. Roll the thin colored paper into balls and place on top of the cones to create different flavors of ice cream.

   Cups: Fold square paper as shown in illustrations (a) to (f), then press on opposite edges until the paper opens up to form a cup. Last, roll the thin colored paper into balls and place in the cups to represent the ice cream.

   ### Cones

## Cups

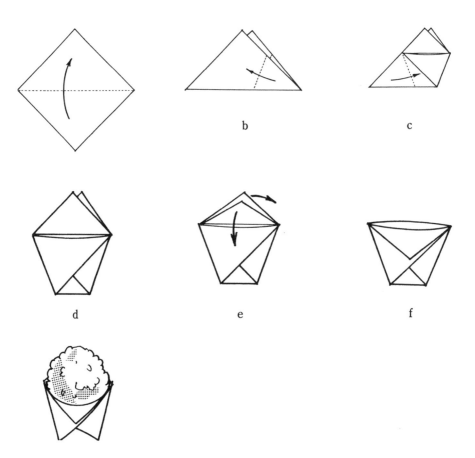

3. Decide on who is going to be the ice-cream vendor and who the customer, and do a role-play. Make groups of five or six students, and have them do role-plays simultaneously.

**Advice for the teacher:**

- It is a good idea to decide the number of flavors to be used in the role-plays beforehand, keeping the age and ability of the students in mind. It might be wise to limit the flavors to what is commonly available.

- You might also want to introduce some additional elements and conditions into the role-play, such as having the students work out what to do when the flavor they want is not available, or when the money they have is limited and they have to buy for several people.

**29** WHAT'S THE GROUP?

■ **Level of Japanese:** Beginners
  (intermediate, advanced)
■ **Students' age:** 14 to 18

■ **Required time:** 30 minutes

### AIMS OF THE ACTIVITY

Learning rules governing the conjugation of verbs
by guessing which group verbs belong to

**Important expressions:**

● 何のグループですか (What group does it belong to?)
● ～は何形ですか (What form is it?)

**What the students must already know:**

● Verb conjugations (such as the dictionary form, the *-masu* form and the *-te* form)

**Materials to prepare:**

● Sets of 30 cards (5 cm x 10 cm) showing the dictionary form of verbs learned so far (excluding する and 来る)

**Procedure:**

1. Divide the class into groups of 3 to 4.
2. Give each group a set of 30 verb cards.
3. Each group divides its cards into groups of *-u* verbs and *-ru* verbs.
4. The teacher introduces new verbs, and the students must guess which category of verb they belong to.

**Advice for the teacher:**

● By means of this activity, *-u* verbs and *-ru* verbs can be introduced to the students.
● The verb cards can be made by the teacher or by the students themselves.
● By looking at verbs already learned from a new angle, this activity is useful when you come to teach the verb forms used for expressing "can" (e.g., 食べられる) and "want" (e.g., 食べたい).

## 30 SUGOROKU WITH NUMBERS

- ■ **Level of Japanese:** Beginners (intermediate, advanced)
- ■ **Students' age:** 6 to 10
- ■ **Required time:** 15 to 20 minutes

---

### AIMS OF THE ACTIVITY

Practicing words and relating them to their meanings

---

**Important expressions:**

● ～さんの番です。

**What the students must already know:**

● How to ask and answer simple questions, and the names of things

**Materials to prepare:**

● A board game with a number in every square on the board.

Example of a sugoroku board with numbers:

● One die

● Enough markers for the number of players (markers should be individually differentiated)

● Question cards numbered to match the numbers on the board

**Procedure:**

1. Divide the class into groups of 4 or 5, and have them sit in a circle.

2. Put the pieces on ふりだし (the starting point), and decide who will go first (doing paper, scissors or stone). The first player rolls the die.

3. The player moves his or her piece forward the number of squares represented by the roll of the die, and reads the question card for that square.

   Examples of question cards:

   この部屋にある物を4つ言ってください。

   やおやさんにあるものを5つ言ってください。

   今日のお天気はどうですか。

4. If the player is able to answer the question correctly, their marker stays on its new square. If unable to answer the question, the player must follow the instructions written on the card.

Examples of instructions written on the cards:

犬（猫）の鳴き声を日本語で言う。

「ふりだし」に戻る。

1回休み。

教室の中をスキップで1周する。

となりの人とじゃんけんをして勝ったら、3コマ進み、負けたら3コマ戻る。

日本語で早口ことばを言う。

5. The first player to reach the end（あがり）is the winner.

**Advice for the teacher:**

- If there are fewer than 10 students in the class, you can do this activity as a class, or you can divide them into groups and have them put their desks together.
- You can also have the students make their own boards, but rather than using question cards, they follow the directions given on the board and have fun speaking Japanese as they play the game.

Example of a sugoroku made by a student:

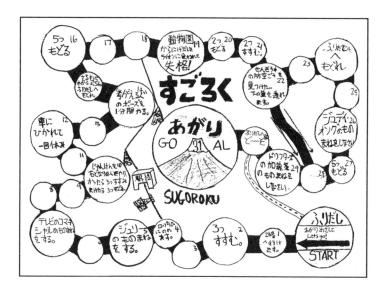

**Appendix:**

- Sugoroku board game with numbers

## 31 SUGOROKU WITH PARTICLES

■ **Level of Japanese:** Beginners
  (intermediate, advanced)
■ **Students' age:** all

■ **Required time:** 15 to 20 minutes

### AIMS OF THE ACTIVITY

## Making sentences using particles

**Important expressions:**

● ～さんの番です (It's ~'s turn.)

**What the students must already know:**

● The basic use of particles

**Materials to prepare:**

● A board game with a particle in every square on the board

● One die

● Enough markers for the number of players (individually differentiated)

**Procedure:**

1. Divide the class into groups of 4 or 5, and have them sit in a circle.
2. Put the pieces on ふりだし (the starting point), and decide who will go first (doing paper, scissors or stone). The first player rolls the die.
3. The player moves his or her marker forward the number of squares represented by the roll of the die, and makes a sentence using the particle written on the square the piece lands on.
4. If the player is able to make a correct sentence, their piece stays on its new square. If not, it returns to its old square.
5. The first player to reach the end is the winner.

**Advice for the teacher:**

● Make sure the students know that particles can be used in more than one way.

**Appendix:**

● Sugoroku board with particles

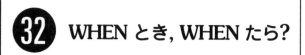

**32** # WHEN とき, WHEN たら?

- ■**Level of Japanese:** Beginners (intermediate, advanced)
- ■**Students' age:** 11 to 18
- ■**Required time:** 30 minutes

## AIMS OF THE ACTIVITY

### Using ～とき and ～たら

**Important expressions:**

- ●～とき（when）
- ●～たら（if）
- ●誰でしょう（Who is it?）

**What the students must already know:**

- How to form complete sentences

**Materials to prepare:**

- One worksheet for every student

Example 1:

なまえ: _____。

1. Noun
こどものとき、_____。

2. *-I* adjective
頭が痛いとき、_____。

3. *Na* adjective
ひまなとき、_____。

4. Dictionary form
がっこうにくるとき、_____。

5. *-Ta* form
しゅくだいをわすれたとき、_____。

6. _____ とき、_____。

Example 2:

なまえ:

1. しゅくだいをわすれたら、_____。
2. 1万円をひろったら、_____。
3. 大きくなったら、_____。
4. 日本にしょうたいされたら、_____。
5. 21せいきになったら、_____。

**Procedure:**

1. Give each student a worksheet.
2. The students think of how to complete the sentences and write their answers on the worksheet.
3. After a stipulated time is up, the worksheets are collected. The teacher or the students read out one worksheet at a time, and the class guesses who wrote what.

**Advice for the teacher:**

• This activity works best (is most fun) with a large number of students.

## 33 DEPARTMENT STORE

■**Level of Japanese:** Beginners
(intermediate, advanced)

■**Students' age:** 8 to 13

■**Required time:** 30 minutes

### AIMS OF THE ACTIVITY

Practicing words and relating them to their meanings

**Important expressions:**

- 〜はどこにありますか （Where is ~?）
- 〜は〜階にあります （~ is on the ~th floor.）
- 地下1階、1階、2階、3階、4階、5階、6階、7階、8階 （or はっかい）、屋上

**What the students must already know:**

- The names of things sold in department stores

**Materials to prepare:**

- Photocopies of the illustration showing what is sold on each floor of a department store (appendix). Photocopies of the outline of a department store (appendix).

**Procedure:**

1. Study the first picture of the department store as a class.

2. Students write down what they want and make a shopping list.

3. Decide who is going to play the part of the receptionist at the information desk and who is going to be the customer.

4. The customer looks at his or her shopping list and asks the receptionist 〜は何階にありますか (Which floor is ~ on?)

5. The receptionist gives the appropriate floor: 〜は〜階にあります (~ is on the ~th floor).

6. Students write down on the department store outline what they will buy on which floor, and complete their shopping plan of action.

**Advice for the teacher:**

- Japanese department stores tend to have similar floor plans, and here the students can study one such example.

- It can also be fun for students to compare the cultural differences between Japanese department stores and those in their own countries.

- You might mention that in the real world receptionists are more likely to use the more polite ございます rather than the plain あります (e.g., 〜は3階にございます) or they might specify the section of a floor (e.g., 〜は3階の婦人服売場にございます).

**Appendices 1:**

- Illustration of a department store showing what is on sale on each floor.
- Illustration of a department store left blank for students to write on.

| **34** **FIVE-WORD GAMES** | ■**Level of Japanese:** Beginners (intermediate, advanced) ■**Students' age:** all ■**Required time:** 15 minutes |
| --- | --- |

## AIMS OF THE ACTIVITY

Review of particles / Making simple sentences

**Important expressions:**

● Expressions for indicating "Who does what, when and where": いつ、どこで、だれが、何を、します

**What the students must already know:**

● To be able to read and write sentences of the type いつ、どこで、だれが、何を、します (Who does what, when and where).

**Materials to prepare:**

● White cards the size of playing cards (each student will need five cards)

**Procedure:**

1. The teacher writes the following on the blackboard:

1. いつ　　　2. どこで　　　3. だれが　　　4. 何を　　　5. します。

2. The teacher gives each student five cards.

3. The students write the numbers from 1 to 5 on the cards, then write words corresponding to the above categories on each card, so forming a sentence.

4. The teacher collects the cards from the students, keeping the five categories separate, and shuffles each category.

5. The teacher gives five students five cards from each category to read.

6. The five students read the cards in their numerical order.

**Advice for the teacher:**

● This activity works best with classes of less than 15 students.

● Even if the words written on the cards by the students are prosaic, shuffling the cards creates some bizarre and humorous juxtapositions, which should get the class laughing. At the same time students will also be consolidating their knowledge of sentence structure and particle usage. Finally the teacher might also like to have the class decide which of the five constructed sentences was the funniest.

● As a variation on this game, the teacher can add a sixth card, on which the students must write "with whom" something was done:

1. いつ　　　2 どこで　　　3 だれが　　　4 だれと　　　5 何を　　　　　6 します。

For example:

| 毎日 | プールで | マイクが | ねこと | しゅくだいを | します。 |
| --- | --- | --- | --- | --- | --- |
| Everyday | at the pool | Mike | with a cat | homework | does. |

● By giving the students different patterns to follow (that is, by having them read the cards in a different order), you can draw their attention to the fact that Japanese word order is not rigid.

**WHICH PERSON IS IT?**

■ **Level of Japanese:** Beginners (intermediate, advanced), Intermediate
■ **Students' age:** all

■ **Required time:** 20 minutes

## AIMS OF THE ACTIVITY

Practicing words and relating them to their meanings

**Important expressions:**

● 背が高いです / 背が低いです (tall / short)
● 太っています / やせています (plump or fat / thin)
● めがねをかけています / めがねをかけていません (is wearing / isn't wearing glasses)
● 髪が茶色です / 髪が黒です (has brown / black hair)
● 笑っています (is laughing, smiling)
● この人です (It's this person)
● 右から〜人目 / 〜番目の人です (It's the 〜st person from the right.)
● 1人目、2人目、3人目、4人目、5人目、6人目、7人目、8人目、9人目、10人目
● 1番目、2番目、3番目、4番目、5番目、6番目、7番目、8番目、9番目、10番目

**What the students must already know:**

● How to describe physical characteristics

**Materials to prepare:**

● Ask students to bring family or group photographs from home

**Procedure:**

1. Split the class into groups. Make sure the members of a group can all clearly see the same photo.
2. Choose one person in each group to describe one of the people in the photo.
3. The chosen student shows the rest of the group the photo and describes 3 to 5 characteristics of a given person in the picture.
4. The other members of the group must guess which person in the photo is being described.

**Advice for the teacher:**

● Using phrases or sentences that are suitable for the students' level of Japanese, talk about people's characteristics.

● Using family photos the students have brought from home, talk about the people in the photos: their clothes, their facial expressions, what jobs they might do, what hobbies they might have, etc. This will expand the range of expressions beyond what was covered in the class.

● Many Japanese have the same color eyes and hair. It can be fun to see how people are described (and what expressions are used) on the missing persons posters often found in train stations, or in the announcements made over the intercom in department stores for children who have gotten separated from their parents.

**36** LET'S MAKE SENTENCES

■ **Level of Japanese:** Beginners
  (intermediate, advanced)
■ **Students' age:** all

■ **Required time:** 15 minutes

## AIMS OF THE ACTIVITY

Learning verb forms (conjugations)

**Important expressions:**

• None

**What the students must already know:**

• How to conjugate verbs

**Materials to prepare:**

• Sentences with the verbs omitted

**Procedure:**

1. Choose which verb form is to be studied, and tell the class:

   e.g.: きょうは、ます形（た形、辞書形）を使いましょう (Today we are going to use the *-masu* form [the *-ta* form or the dictionary form].)

2. Divide the class into groups of 3.

3. One member of each group collects a sheet of questions from the teacher. In each question the verb is missing.

   E.g.: トム君は算数を＿＿＿＿＿＿。(Tom ＿＿＿＿ arithmetic.)

4. The student tells the other two members of the group what the question is.

5. The two students think of a suitable verb to complete the sentence, and each writes down the answer on a piece of paper.

6. At a sign from the teacher, the students show their answers.

**Advice for the teacher:**

• You might want to have the groups compete against one another. For example, if the two students both write the same answer, that can count as one point for their group, but if their answers are different, they get no points (even if their answers happen to be correct). Making it into a game like this where points are won and lost without reference to students' Japanese ability ensures everyone can have fun. No one is left feeling inadequate because their Japanese isn't up to scratch.

| **37** CAN YOU SEE IT? | ■ **Level of Japanese:** Beginners (intermediate, advanced)<br>■ **Students' age:** 8 to 18<br><br>■ **Required time:** 20 to 45 minutes |
|---|---|

| AIMS OF THE ACTIVITY |
|---|
| Practicing relating words to their meanings |

**Important expressions:**

- どこがあいていますか （Which side is open?）
  上、下、右、左、ななめ上、ななめ下 （above, below, right, left, on a slant above, on a slant below.）
- これはなんですか （What is this?）
- これを読んでください （Read this [when using hiragana or katakana on the eye chart]）
  読めません （I can't.）

**What the students must already know:**

- Expressions of place and position
- How to read hiragana and katakana
- Verbal expressions in the potential negative form

**Materials to prepare:**

- An eye test form (see appendix)
- An eye chart (see appendix)
- A pointer (e.g., a pencil or a ruler)
- Something to cover one eye (e.g., a ladle or spoon)

**Procedure:**

1. Enlarge the eye chart and stick it on the blackboard or an easel.
2. Divide the class into groups of 3.
3. Decide in each group who is going to take the test, who is going to conduct it, and who is going to write down the results.
4. The student conducting the test points to the letters on the eye chart and asks これはなんですか or says これを読んでください. Pointing to the middle row of circles with an opening on one side, the student conducting the test asks, どこがあいていますか.
5. The student conducting the eye test and the student recording the results decide how good their classmate's eyesight is, based on the number of answers he or she got correct.
6. The results of the test are recorded on the eye test form and reported to the student whose eyes were tested.
7. In the area on the form where it says Observations （かんさつ）, comments such as よく見えます, よく読めます, and たいへんよくできました can be written.

**Advice for the teacher:**

- At any one time, only 3 or at the very most 4 or 5 students can do the activity together, so prepare enough materials so that everyone can take part. Alternatively you can have just one group do the activity, and have the rest of the class watch.
- You can also do this activity with an eye chart using kanji (instead of kana). At the top of the chart write easy characters, making them more difficult as you work your way down the chart.

**Appendix:**

- Eye test form
- Eye chart

# 38 MAKE YOUR OWN MENU

■ **Level of Japanese:** Beginners (advanced)

■ **Students' age:** 8 to 10

■ **Required time:** 20 minutes

## AIMS OF THE ACTIVITY

Learning expressions useful in a restaurant
by making menus and using them in role-plays

**Important expressions:**

● ひとつ、1本、一人前、定食、飲み物 (one, one bottle, one serving, set course, drinks)

**What the students must already know:**

● How to write the names of food and drinks

● The names and types of food (including Japanese)

● The approximate price of food and drink

**Materials to prepare:**

● Thick paper for making a menu (it can be colored)

**Procedure:**

1. Divide the class into groups of 5 or 6.

2. Each group decides what kind of food the restaurant will serve (fast food, Japanese food, Chinese, Italian, Thai, etc.)

3. Decide the name of the restaurant, the items on the menu, and the prices. Each group should make different choices.

4. Make the menu, writing in large letters.

5. Do a role-play using the menu: for example, two to four friends or a family going out for a meal. It might be fun to use the plastic samples seen in some restaurants if you can get hold of any.

**Advice for the teacher:**

● Making the menu on a computer will give you much room for creativity.

● It is a good idea to bring to class some examples of real menus used in restaurants (and if Japanese, all the better!). You can show them to the class using an overhead projector or pass them around so everyone can get a close look. If you bring a real menu to class, you can also have the class talk about the following :

(1) 4人家族が7000円の予算で外食をしたいと思います。あなたなら、何を注文しますか。

(2) 日本と〜との食事の値段を比べてみましょう。

(3) 〜 (name of country or 〜さんの国) では食べる前に／食べた後に何か言いますか。

● When doing the role-plays, the keywords and expressions that need to be practiced are:

いらっしゃいませ、いただきます、ごちそうさまでした

お水／おひや（おはし、おしぼり、ナイフ、フォーク、おしょうゆ、ソース）をください

## 39

**PAPER SLIDES**

■ **Level of Japanese:** Beginners (advanced), Intermediate
■ **Students' age:** all

■ **Required time:** 45 to 90 minutes

## AIMS OF THE ACTIVITY

Writing and understanding the construction (composition)
of stories that take place over a period of time

**Important expressions:**

● 〜時〜分（~ hours and ~ minutes）
● 始めに／まず、次に／そして、最後に／やがて（First [first of all], next [and then], last [finally])
● ある日、そして、ところが、そこで（one day, then, but, and then）

**What the students must already know:**

● How to write simple sentences

**Materials to prepare:**

● Thick paper to make paper slides

**Procedure:**

1. Show the whole class a previously prepared paper slide.

2. Divide the class into groups of 4 or 5.

3. Each group thinks of a story and 4 pictures to illustrate the story.

4. Each group makes their paper slides.

5. When they have finished making their paper slides, they show them to the class.

6. The class writes down each group's story.

**Advice for the teacher:**

● It takes time to make the paper slides, but once you have made them, you can use them again and again. This activity is a useful and effective way of explaining expressions relating to the passage of time.

● Here are some examples of stories that take place over a period of time:

Example 1:
太郎君が生まれました。
幼稚園生になりました。
小学生になりました。
中学生になりました。

Example 2:
なんの卵でしょう。
音がします。象かな。かいじゅうかな。
ことこと動いています。象かな。
あっ、割れた。ひよこが出てきた。

Example 3:
7:00　起きます。
7:05　さあ、朝ごはんですよ。
7:15　そして、歯磨きをします。
7:45　行ってきます。

Example of a paper slide:

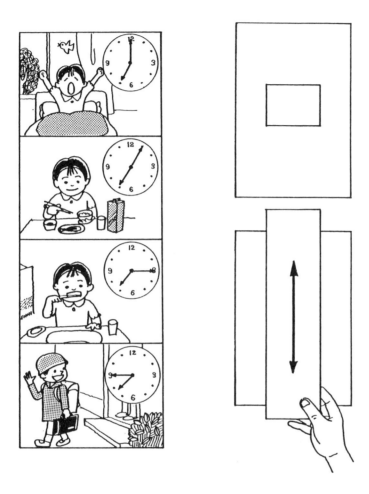

| | |
|---|---|
| **40** **HOW ABOUT SATURDAY?** | ■ **Level of Japanese:** Beginners (advanced), Intermediate<br>■ **Students' age:** 11 to 18<br><br>■ **Required time:** 20 to 30 minutes |

## AIMS OF THE ACTIVITY

### Negotiating with someone to decide on a time

**Important expressions:**

● 〜ませんか （Would you ~?)
● 〜曜日（〜日、〜時）はどうですか （How about ~day [date, time]?)
● いいですね （That sounds fine.)
● ちょっとだめです （I'm afraid it's no good.)
● 〜曜日（〜日、〜時）にしましょう （Let's make it ~day [date, time].)

**What the students must already know:**

● Expressions of time (the days of the week, dates, and how to tell the time)
● Expressions for things to do or places to go on weekends

**Materials to prepare:**

● One worksheet for every student (see appendix)

**Procedure:**

1. Divide the class into pairs.
2. Give all the students a worksheet.
3. The teacher gives the class a topic or topics.
4. In pairs the students discuss when to meet, and decide on a day and a time.
5. They tell the rest of the class what they have decided.

**Advice for the teacher:**

● With students of beginner level it is a good idea for the teacher to write their schedules on their worksheets for them.
● Depending on the students' level you might want to give them more difficult topics. For example, the student council is planning a dance. The class must decide when to hold the committee meetings for the dance and when to hold the dance itself, fitting them in with the school calendar. Alternatively, you might have them decide when a group of friends will go and see a movie.
● Depending on the students' level, you might want to teach them how to talk with someone older than themselves about making plans and appointments (e.g., how to tell someone that the time suggested to meet is not convenient). You might also teach them useful expressions for deciding such matters over the telephone.

**Appendix:**

● Schedule worksheet

**41 THE SHOPPING GAME**

■ **Level of Japanese:** Beginners
   (advanced), Intermediate
■ **Students' age:** 6 to 13

■ **Required time:** 15 to 20 minutes

## AIMS OF THE ACTIVITY

Learning how to go shopping by doing role-plays

**Important expressions:**

● いらっしゃいませ （Please come in.)
● （〜は〜で）いくらですか （How much is ~ [number] ~ [objects]?)
● （〜で）〜円です （For ~ [number] it is ~ yen.)
● 毎度ありがとうございます （Thank you for coming in so often.)

**What the students must already know:**

● Expressions used when shopping

**Materials to prepare:**

● Picture cards showing items sold in stores (e.g., cards showing pictures of egg-plants, cucumbers, and other vegetables sold in a grocery store)
● A large bag or basket in which to put the cards of items bought
● Play money (Japanese yen)
● Cards showing prices

**Procedure:**

1. Divide the class into groups of 5 to 6 students.
2. In each group the students decide who will be the clerk, with the rest customers.
3. The clerk lines up the picture cards showing items on sale, decides how much they cost, and places price cards in front of them.
4. The customer and the clerk act out a role-play.

**Advice for the teacher:**

● You might want to use plastic models instead of the picture cards to represent the items on sale.

 **BINGO**

| | |
|---|---|
| | ■ **Level of Japanese:** all levels |
| | ■ **Students' age:** all |
| | ■ **Required time:** 20 to 40 minutes |

## AIMS OF THE ACTIVITY

### Having fun learning words and letters

**Important expressions:**

- できました！(Finished!)
- たて (vertically, up and down), よこ (horizontally, across), ななめ (diagonally), コの字型 horizontal U-shape, バツ（×）型 x-shape

**What the students must already know:**

- How to read the hiragana, katakana or kanji used in the activity

**Materials to prepare:**

- A bingo card for every player (each card being different)
- Letter cards (small pieces of paper, cardboard, etc. with hiragana, katakana, or kanji written on them)
- Markers (things such as poker chips or beans)

**Procedure:**

1. Decide on the shape (pattern) in which the markers are to be put down in order to win: e.g., たて (vertically, up and down), よこ (horizontally, across), ななめ (diagonally), コの字型 horizontal U-shape, バツ（×）型 x-shape.

2. Put the pieces of paper with letters on them into a box or bowl to be drawn out one at a time at random.

3. Either the teacher or a student draws a card.

4. As the letters are called out, the students put down markers on their cards if the letter called out happens to be there.

5. The first student to complete the correct shape shouts, できました (Finished!).

**Advice for the teacher:**

- Making the bingo cards takes time, but once made, you can use them again and again. If you choose a good quality paper, they will last a long time.
- Depending on the students' level, you can adapt the bingo game in many ways. For example: hiragana bingo, katakana bingo, kanji bingo (numbers in kanji, personal or family names, place-names, etc.), theme bingo (family relations, names of classroom objects, academic subjects [math etc.], names of foods, etc.).

Examples of bingo cards:

| で | き | ま | し | た |
|---|---|---|---|---|
| ね | に | さ | う | て |
| ち | か | そ | た | く |
| あ | す | け | こ | な |
| の | し | つ | い | せ |
| え | し | き | ぬ | お |

| で | き | ま | し | た |
|---|---|---|---|---|
| すいか | にく | かさ | いぬ | おの |
| たいこ | なに | くち | ねこ | おに |
| とけい | て | ✕ | いえ | うそ |
| ちかい | しか | かき | そこ | あさ |
| けいと | なし | つき | うえ | あせ |

| で | き | ま | し | た |
|---|---|---|---|---|
| ニャー | シャー | ティン | ション | ビュッ |
| チャッ | ピュー | ジョン | リュー | シュー |
| フェア | ジェ | キャッ | フォー | チョ |
| ディー | ショー | ニュー | シュッ | リュッ |
| キャー | フィン | チュー | ミュー | チョッ |

| で | き | ま | し | た |
|---|---|---|---|---|
| 三十九 | 七 | 三十五 | 七十 | 一 |
| 十四 | 四十八 | 九十一 | 二十六 | 五十二 |
| 六十二 | 三十一 | ✕ | 六十三 | 八十七 |
| 八十六 | 七十七 | 九十九 | 三十八 | 二十五 |
| 十三 | 四十 | 三十一 | 七十九 | 五十三 |

<table>
<tr><td>

**43** **WHERE'S THE MISTAKE?**

</td><td>

■ **Level of Japanese:** all levels

■ **Students' age:** all

■ **Required time:** 5 to 10 minutes

</td></tr>
</table>

### AIMS OF THE ACTIVITY

Focusing on words that are wrong / Warm-up activity

**Important expressions:**

• None

**What the students must already know:**

• Nothing in particular

**Materials to prepare:**

• Choose what you are going to focus on from the various areas you have covered so far: words, sentences, sentence patterns, grammatical points, questions of accent (stress) and intonation, etc.

• Write on the blackboard a word or sentence containing one or more mistakes.

Examples: えんぱつ

わたしわいぬをすちです。

エリザベスを見れば、知らせてください。

**Procedure:**

1. As soon as the students enter the classroom, they must find the mistakes in the sentences written on the blackboard, and write the correct version in their notebooks.

Examples: えんぴつ

わたしはいぬがすきです。

エリザベスを見たら、知らせてください。

2. When everyone has finished, check the answers.

**Advice for the teacher:**

• In the early stages it might be best to tell the class how many mistakes there are in each sentence.

• In the early stages it might be best to work on only one point at a time (e.g., particles), writing three or four sentences for each one. For example:

いぬですきです。

すいかにたべます。

水へのみたい。

• It is a good idea to choose mistakes that have appeared in students' written and spoken work.

• This activity can also be used for teaching stress and intonation. The teacher reads a sentence putting the stress in the wrong places, and gets the class to correct the mistakes. For example, the teacher says: わた̲しは いぬ̲が す̲きです (where the underlined syllables are stressed). The class corrects this, saying: わた̲しは いぬ̲が す̲きです。

| **44** THE MAGIC WORD | ■ **Level of Japanese:** all levels |
| | ■ **Students' age:** all |
| | ■ **Required time:** not applicable |

## AIMS OF THE ACTIVITY

### Encouraging students to speak Japanese

**Important expressions:**

● None

**What the students must already know:**

● Nothing in particular

**Materials to prepare:**

● None

**Procedure:**

1. The teacher says 日本語です, and everyone claps their hands. A magic spell is cast and only Japanese can now be spoken!

2. The teacher says 英語です (or whatever language is the students' mother tongue), everyone claps their hands, and the magic spell is broken. The students can speak their mother tongue again.

**Advice for the teacher:**

● This is one way to make the class speak as much Japanese as possible and prevent them from reverting to their mother tongue.

● The ultimate goal of the activity is to have the magic last the whole class from beginning to end (i.e., the class only speaks Japanese).

● You must make it absolutely clear that the teacher is the only one able to work the magic spell (and then break it).

● To help the students to relax and get used to this activity, it is best to start off with short spells of 2 to 3 minutes.

● You might want to use a small notice showing the class when the magic is working and when it is not, and which language is to be used (see below).

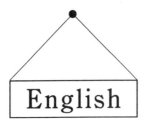

# 45 LET'S WRITE HAIKU

- **Level of Japanese:** Intermediate
- **Students' age:** 11 to 18
- **Required time:** 45 minutes

## AIMS OF THE ACTIVITY

Learning the order of Subject + Object + Predicate
with the haiku rhythm of 5 syllables + 7 syllables + 5 syllables

**Important expressions:**

● None

**What the students must already know:**

● Use of particles

**Materials to prepare:**

● Worksheet divided into 5-7-5 structure (see appendix)

**Procedure:**

1. Explain what haiku are and how to write them.

2. Introduce some examples of haiku, explaining the 5-7-5 structure, the subject + object + predicate order, and the use of particles.

| | | |
|---|---|---|
| にほんごの | かんじとじょしは | むずかしい |
| 寄せる波 | 私の足に | ごあいさつ |
| 赤とんぼ | 夕やけ空と | 同じいろ |
| 見いつけた！ | エビのかくれた | さんごしょう |

3. Students try to write their own haiku, sticking to the 5-7-5 syllable structure.

4. Students write a fair copy of their haiku on the worksheet provided in the appendix. Use one square of the worksheet for each syllable. Thus じょ is written all in one square.

5. Students explain their haiku to the rest of the class.

**Advice for the teacher:**

● In the introductory explanation about haiku the teacher should mention *kigo* (the seasonal words) and the other basic conventions involved in writing haiku. However, when students practice writing their own haiku, do not stick too rigidly to any set of rules. Let the students experiment freely.

● With advanced classes it can be fun to learn about *kigo* and onomatopoeia.

● It might be interesting to link up with the art class and get the students to draw pictures illustrating their haiku.

● Exhibiting the students' work in the classroom or making it into a book is sure to please them.

**Appendix:**

● Worksheet

Reference:

● Jambor, Kinuko A. (ed.). *A Chorus of Haiku*. Kobe, Japan: Marist Brothers International School, 1993

| **46** THE READING TREE | ■ **Level of Japanese:** Intermediate, Advanced<br>■ **Students' age:** all<br><br>■ **Required time:** 20 to 40 minutes |

## AIMS OF THE ACTIVITY

Getting students interested in books
by having them read stories and write their opinions

**Important expressions:**

● None

**What the students must already know:**

● Nothing in particular

**Materials to prepare:**

● Green pieces of paper about 15 cm square cut into the shape of a leaf (see appendix).

● The trunk and branches of a paper tree to be stuck on a classroom wall or noticeboard.

**Procedure:**

1. Students choose a book to read.

2. After reading the book, students write the title (本の題名), the author (作者), their opinion of the book (感想), and their own name (名前) on a piece of green leaf-shaped paper.

3. When they have finished writing, students tell the class what they have written.

4. Students attach their completed leaves to the tree on the classroom wall.

**Advice for the teacher:**

● If the chosen books are too difficult, students will not get a sense of achievement from reading them. It is a good idea for the teacher to advise students on the choice of a suitable book.

**Recommended books:**

● The following list is primarily aimed at elementary school children, but it should also prove useful for junior high and high school students. For the latter age the Iwanami Junior series is also highly recommended.

**Intermediate:**

● キンダーおはなしえほん（フレーベル館）*Kindā ohanashi ehon* (Furēberu-kan)

● おはなし絵本館（講談社）*Ohanashi ehon-kan* (Kōdansha)

● むかしばなしシリーズ（講談社）*Mukashi-banashi shirīzu* (Kōdansha)

**Advanced:**

● 日本の名作文庫シリーズ（ポプラ社）*Nihon no meisaku bunko shirīzu* (Popurasha)

● フォア文庫（金の星社）*Fuoa bunko* (Kin no Hoshisha)

● 青い鳥文庫（講談社）*Aoi tori bunko* (Kōdansha)

● 偕成社文庫（偕成社）*Kaiseisha bunko* (Kaiseisha)

● 光村読書シリーズ1年から6年（光村教育図書）*Mitsumura dokusho shirīzu* (Mitsumura Kyōiku Tosho)

• If students are unable to write their opinions in Japanese, make a questionnaire suitable for their age and Japanese ability, on which students circle the answer that most closely fits their opinion.

     E.g.: この本は　　おもしろかった
                つまらなかった
                長すぎた
                短すぎた

(This book was interesting / boring / too long / too short.)

**Appendix:**

• Tree leaf

 **PENCIL TALK**

■ **Level of Japanese:** Intermediate, Advanced

■ **Students' age:** all

■ **Required time:** 15 to 20 minutes

## AIMS OF THE ACTIVITY

Asking each other questions, getting new information,
and putting it into written form

**Important expressions:**

● None

**What the students must already know:**

● How to write hiragana, at the very least

**Materials to prepare:**

● One worksheet for each pair (see appendix)

**Procedure:**

1. Split up into pairs, one student being A, the other B (or they can use their own initials instead).
2. No talking is allowed.
3. Choose a subject (e.g., my pets, your pets, plans for this coming Sunday, what was done last Sunday, my family, your family). Students ask each other questions (and answer them) using only pencil and paper (see next page, top). No talking allowed.
4. Each student writes an essay about their partner based on what they have learned (see next page, bottom).

**Advice for the teacher:**

● This activity can be an effective way of helping students to get to know each other and make friends at the start of the school year.

● Make sure that both students in each pair ask and answer an equal number of questions.

● The essays need not be very long.

● It can be fun to have pairs tell the class what they wrote about each other.

**Appendix:**

● Worksheet

Examples of students' compositions:

**48** **COMIC STRIPS**

■ **Level of Japanese:** Intermediate, Advanced
■ **Students' age:** 8 to 18

■ **Required time:** 45 to 90 minutes

## AIMS OF THE ACTIVITY

Practicing conversation style and conversation development techniques

**Important expressions:**

● None

**What the students must already know:**

● Colloquial expressions

**Materials to prepare:**

● Comic strip worksheets

● Overhead projector (or a noticeboard)

**Procedure:**

1. Looking at an example of a comic strip, the students analyze its component parts and talk about the characters and situations they get into, the historical background, the point of view or perspective, and the humor.

2. Choose a subject that has some relation to what has been studied so far, and the students think of a comic strip to illustrate it.

3. On the worksheet draw the four pictures that will make up the comic strip. It is a good idea to leave this to students who like drawing. Alternatively, have students draw one picture each.

4. Using the overhead projector (or the noticeboard), show the completed comic strip to the whole class.

**Advice for the teacher:**

● You might also try providing the group with just the first picture of the comic strip and having them draw the remaining three.

● When you are running short of time, you can give the class a comic strip that has had its speech balloons whited out, and get them to write their own lines to go in the empty spaces (see examples 1 to 3 on opposite page).

● According to the number of students and the type of class, you can also have them work in pairs or small groups, or alternatively in conjunction with the art class.

● Taking each frame as one scene of a story, have the students write the story behind each scene in place of writing the dialogue.

● You can show the class, and discuss, comic strips that deal with such topics as studying for exams, language and society, social problems, and the function of the family.

• Four examples of the *Fuji Santarō* comic strip drawn by Satō Sampei and published in the *Asahi Shimbun* newspaper on (1) 1/19/79, (2) 1/3/90, (3) 5/29/91, (4) 7/17/90.

**References:**

• Recommend comic strips:
  コボちゃん (*Kobo-chan*), くもんお話カード (*Kumon ohanashi kādo*), サザエさん (*Sazae-san*), フジ三太郎 (*Fuji Santarō*)

• Available books:
  文庫版『ササエさん』45巻　長谷川町子（朝日新聞社 1994-95）(*Sazae-san* by Hasegawa Machiko [Asahi Shimbun 1994-95])

  『対訳サザエさん』12巻　長谷川町子（講談社インターナショナル 1997-）(*The Wonderful World of Sazae-san*, by Machiko Hasegawa. Kodansha International, 1997-)

  文庫版『フジ三太郎名場面』19巻　サトウサンペイ（朝日新聞社 1982-91）*Fuji Santarō* by Satō Sampei (Asahi Shimbun 1982-91)

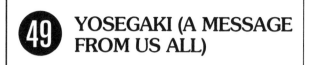

# 49 YOSEGAKI (A MESSAGE FROM US ALL)

- **Level of Japanese:** Intermediate, Advanced
- **Students' age:** 8 to 13
- **Required time:** 20 to 45 minutes

## AIMS OF THE ACTIVITY

Making short phrases or sentences about given subjects

**Important expressions:**

- None

**What the students must already know:**

- How to write at the phrase or sentence level

**Materials to prepare:**

- Paper (drawing paper, colored paper), marker pens, ball pens

**Procedure:**

1. Together with the class decide on a theme (e.g.: Happiness is ... , Family, Morning, etc.).

2. Design the paper so that everybody in the class can write something about the chosen topic on the paper.

3. Leave the paper in one part of the classroom, and have the class write their comments on the paper one by one in their free time or at a time designated by the teacher.

**Advice for the teacher:**

- In Japan it is customary for a number of people to write their messages (or simply sign their names) on one piece of paper or a card to be given to someone in the hospital or for a friend who is about to change schools. These cards are called よせがき.

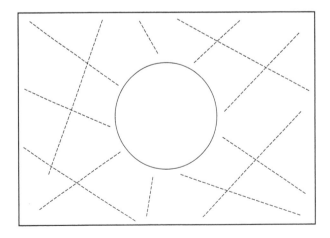

Yosegaki example:

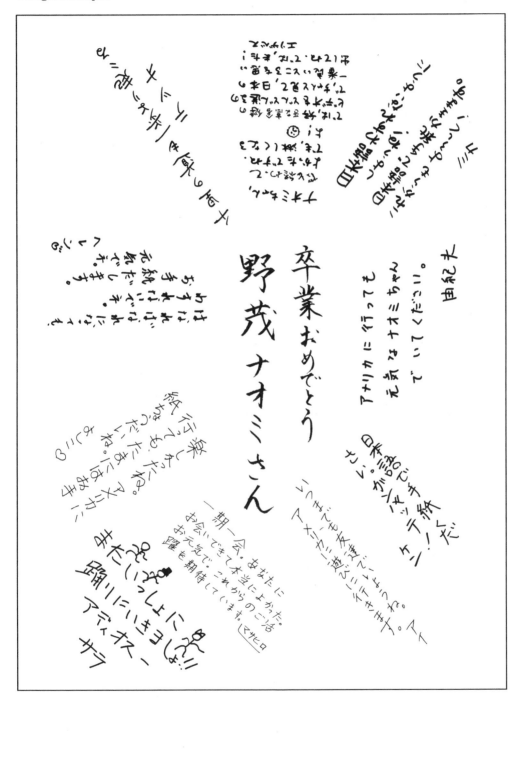

# 50 MAKING PICTURE BOOKS FROM ONE SHEET OF PAPER

■ **Level of Japanese:** Advanced

■ **Students' age:** 8 to 18

■ **Required time:** 30 to 45 minutes

## AIMS OF THE ACTIVITY

Learning to structure and develop stories by scenes

**Important expressions:**

● None

**What the students must already know:**

● How to write sentences

**Materials to prepare:**

● Drawing paper or any other cuttable paper, crayons, marker pens, scissors

● Scratch paper for writing out stories

● Picture books or picture dictionary to be used for reference

**Procedure:**

1. Choose an interesting event (or person) from the material being studied and discuss it as a class.

2. Divide the class into groups.

3. Each group focuses on a subject and breaks it down into eight scenes.

4. Each group writes a rough draft for eight scenes.

5. Each group discusses which scenes should be illustrated and how they should be illustrated.

6. Making the book

    a) Fold a rectangular piece of paper twice vertically and once horizontally to produce eight equal rectangles.

    b) Cut along centerfold of two squares in middle (indicated in illustration by a solid line).

    c) Fold the paper horizontally once more.

    d) Press against both sides of cut area so that it opens outward.

    e) Keep pressing until the shape shown in the illustration is produced. Then fold all together to make an eight-page book.

7. Create the layout for each page, balancing the pictures with the text.

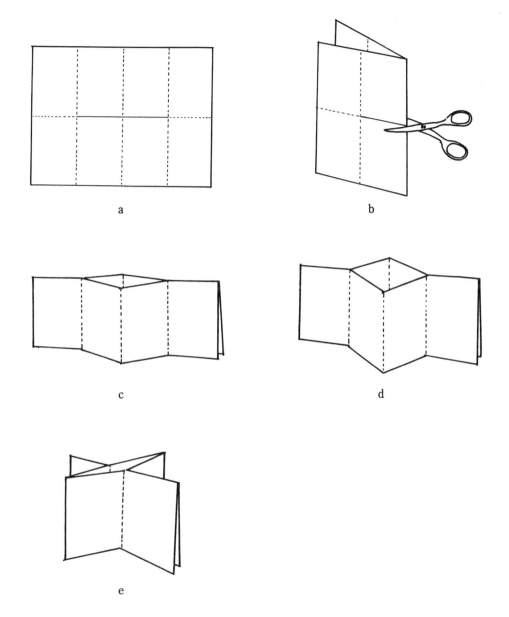

a

b

c

d

e

**Advice for the teacher:**

- You can put the students' books on exhibit or invite students from other classes to come and hear the stories being recited.
- As an alternative, each group can choose a different subject to write about (rather than all the groups the same subject).

**51** THE NEWS WINDOW

- ■**Level of Japanese:** Advanced
- ■**Students' age:** 14 to 18
- ■**Required time:** 5 to 10 minutes

## AIMS OF THE ACTIVITY

Writing down, reporting, and evaluating the contents of the news

**Important expressions:**

- 〜によると、〜そうです (According to ~, ~ happened.)

**What the students must already know:**

- How to understand (more or less) TV and radio programs
- How to read newspapers and magazines

**Materials to prepare:**

- Paper for writing comments (see appendix)

**Procedure:**

1. Choose 2 newscasters for each class.
2. The newscasters each choose a topic and prepare articles on that topic.
3. The newscasters read their articles in front of the class.
4. If time allows, practice question and answer sessions as a class.

**Advice for the teacher:**

- Get the students to choose topics that have recently been in the news.
- It is a good idea to practice this activity once a week on a fixed day.
- You can also have the students evaluate the news and the newscasters, writing their comments on the form provided in the appendix.
- It is necessary to teach the class how to evaluate by showing them some examples. Remind them to write not only critical comments but also positive ones, praising what they liked.

Items for Evaluation (example)

| Content: | 1 | 2 | 3 | 4 | 5 |
|---|---|---|---|---|---|
| Comprehension of the news | | | | | |
| Organization (who, why, when, where, what, and how) | | | | | |

| Presentation: | 1 | 2 | 3 | 4 | 5 |
|---|---|---|---|---|---|
| Clearness of pronunciation | | | | | |
| Voice loud enough | | | | | |
| Pronunciation of end of words clear | | | | | |
| Speed of speaking appropriate | | | | | |

Comments:
    Remarks on the content and presentation

    - - - - - - - - - - - - - - - - - - - - - - - - - - - -
    - - - - - - - - - - - - - - - - - - - - - - - - - - - -
    - - - - - - - - - - - - - - - - - - - - - - - - - - - -

## Appendix:

• Example of an evaluation sheet

# BITS and PIECES

**51 Activities
for Teaching Japanese
K–12**

**①** 暗号ごっこ

## アクティビティのねらい

音声と文字を関連づけ、さらに語彙の意味に結びつける

### 重要な表現
● 特になし

### あらかじめ必要な知識
● 特になし

### 準備するもの
● 学習項目の誤用例

　　例: ごりん　→　りんご

### 進め方

　　① 教師が黒板か紙に単語の文字の順番をかえて書く。

　　② 生徒は正しい順序に訂正する。

### 先生方からのアドバイス

● 日本語は、シラブルが最小単位として表記される言語だということが学べる。

● 授業に入るためのウォーミング・アップとして使える。

 **2 何色カード**

■学習者の
　日本語レベル：初級 (入門)

■学習者の年齢：8才〜13才

■所要時間：5分〜10分

**アクティビティのねらい**

色の表現を練習する

**重要な表現**
●色を表すことば
　〜い (例: 赤い、白い)
　〜の (例: 緑の、むらさきの)

**あらかじめ必要な知識**
●色を表すことば
●いろいろな物の名前

**準備するもの**
●正方形の厚紙の中央に折り紙 (いろいろな色) を貼ったもの (カードA)
●厚紙の中央をいろいろな形に切り抜いたもの (カードB)
　例: かさ、くつ、ふとん (付録参照)

| カードA | カードB |
|---|---|
|  | 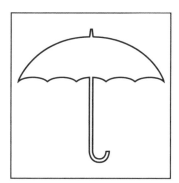 |

**進め方**

① カードAを使って色の名前を学習 (もしくは確認) する。

② カードBを使って物の名前を学習 (もしくは確認) する。

③ カードAの上にカードBを重ね、「赤いかさ」「緑のかさ」と言えるように練習する。

**先生方からのアドバイス**

●慣れるにつれて、カードAとBをパッパと手際よく重ね、つぎつぎと言わせるようにする。

●クラスのウォーミング・アップに使うとよい。

●日頃から学習している名詞の表すものを絵に描き、その形を切り抜いておくとよい。

**付録**

●カードBの形の例

**❸ 魚釣りゲーム**

■学習者の
　日本語レベル：初級（入門）

■学習者の年齢：6才〜8才

■所要時間：15分

## アクティビティのねらい

ことばを聞き、理解する練習をする

### 重要な表現
● 特になし

### あらかじめ必要な知識
● これまでに学習した語彙

### 準備するもの
● クリップをつけた10cm四方の絵カード (5〜6人のグループに10枚ぐらいが適当)

　　　表: 学習した単語の絵

　　　裏: 1点から5点の得点を任意につける。

● U字型の磁石を、ひもでぶらさげた釣竿 (各グループに1本)

### 進め方
　① 5〜6人のグループに分け、グループごとに10枚程度の絵の描かれたカードと
　　　釣竿1本を渡す。
　② グループは輪になり、中央にカードを散らす。
　③ 教師が読み上げる単語のカードを釣る。
　④ 釣り上げたグループは、カードの裏の得点を得る。
　⑤ グループ内で各人が順番に魚釣りをする。
　⑥ ひとまわりした後、得点の多いグループが勝ち。

### 先生方からのアドバイス
● 低学年の生徒たちは魚釣りに夢中になるので、日本語の学習内容も確認する。
● 糸がからむと、ゲームを進めるのに時間がかかるので、糸の長さは50cmくらいま
　でにする。
● 正しいカードを選んで速く釣るにはかなりの集中力がいるので、クリップは軽めに
　しておき、いったん磁石がついたらすぐ釣り上げられるようにしておく。

**④ 仲間集め**

■学習者の
　日本語レベル：初級

■学習者の年齢：特になし

■所要時間：ひとつのテーマ
　　　　　　につき約10分

| アクティビティのねらい |
| --- |
| すでに学習した単語をグループに分け、<br>同じ種類の単語を集めて、語彙の復習をする |

**重要な表現**

●特になし

**あらかじめ必要な知識**

●ひらがな、カタカナの読み書き

**準備するもの**

●1グループにつき1枚の紙

**進め方**

① 2〜4人のグループに分かれ、各自えんぴつを持って車座になる。

② それぞれのグループの真ん中に1枚の紙を置く。

③ 教師はテーマを1つ与える。

　例:「食べもの」「教室にあるもの」「動物」「カタカナことば」「赤いもの」

④ 生徒は、そのカテゴリーに合うことば、また関連のあることばを、限られた
　時間内にできるだけたくさん紙に書く。その際、同じことばを書かないよう
　に、グループ内で相談すること。

⑤ 教師の終了の合図で、生徒はえんぴつを置く。

⑥ ことばをたくさん集めたグループを勝ちとする。

**先生方からのアドバイス**

●なるべく時間を短く区切り、間のびしないようにする。

●グループ別に、書き出したことばを発表してもよい。

●低学年の場合、実物や絵などを使う方法もある。その場合、教室にボール、帽子、
　トマトなどの実物や、模型、絵などを用意しておき、例えば、「丸いもの」という
　テーマを出して生徒に集めさせる。ただし、1人とか2人ずつ順番に動くようにし
　ないと、教室が乱れることがある。

●実物や絵を集めた場合には、「これは何ですか」「トマトです」などとやりとりをする
　こともできる。

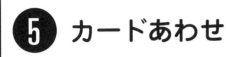

**⑤ カードあわせ**

■学習者の
　日本語レベル：初級

■学習者の年齢：特になし

■所 要 時 間：10分

**アクティビティのねらい**

意味を関連づけながらことばの練習をする

**重要な表現**

● 「だれの番ですか」

● 「わたしの／あなたの／～ (名前) さんの番です」

**あらかじめ必要な知識**

● ひらがな、カタカナ、漢字の読み

**準備するもの**

● 学習している単語の絵を描いたカード

● ひらがな、カタカナ、漢字のうちいずれかのカード

● ジョーカーのカード

**進め方**

① 5～8人のグループに分かれる。

② 生徒は、グループごとに、床の上に車座に座る。

③ 絵カードと文字カードを混ぜて全部配る。

④ じゃんけんなどで順番を決め、隣の人から1枚カードを引いて、絵カードと文字カードが一致したら真ん中にカードを出す。

⑤ 次の人にカードを1枚引いてもらう。

⑥ 早くカードがなくなった人が勝ち。最後にジョーカーを持っていた人が負けとなる。

**先生方からのアドバイス**

● カードの作成にあたって、絵を描くのが難しい場合には、本や教科書のさし絵や写真を切り抜き、カードに貼り付けて作ってもよい。

● カードの枚数が多すぎるとなかなか終わらないので、1グループ5人でカードは30枚以下が適当である。

**⑥ カードで勝負**

■学習者の
　日本語レベル：初級

■学習者の年齢：6才～10才

■所 要 時 間：5分～20分

**アクティビティのねらい**

ことばを読み、発音する

**重要な表現**

●特になし

**あらかじめ必要な知識**

●特になし (ひらがなカードを使う場合はひらがなの読みというように、そのときの
　学習項目を使用)

**準備するもの**

●トランプ程度の大きさのカード

　例　ひらがなカード　　　46枚

　　　動詞カード　　　　　(表にひらがな、裏に絵を描いたもの)

　　　形容詞カード　　　　(表にひらがな、裏に絵を描いたもの)

　　　名詞カード　　　　　(表にひらがな、裏に絵を描いたもの)

(表)

(裏)

**進め方**

    ① 2人でペアになる。

    ② お互いに自分のカードをシャッフルし、左手に重ねたカードを持って、右手で1枚ずつ相手に示す。

    ③ まずカードの表を使って、相手がそのカードに書かれている文字を正しく読め、言えるかどうか練習する。

    ④ もう一度カードをシャッフルし、今度はカードの裏を使って、該当する日本語が言えるかどうか練習する。

**先生方からのアドバイス**

● 1人でめくりながら、自習もできる。

● 2人で競ってもよい。2人のうちでどちらが多く (何分かの制限時間内で何枚読めるか) 、どちらが正しく (与えられたカードのうち正しく読めるのは何枚か) 読めるかなどを競う。この場合、教師、または、別の生徒が判定者となってもよい。

● 2人ずつのペアで対戦していき、クラス全体で勝ち抜きゲームにしてもよい。

● 読み間違えたカードについては何度かくり返してもよい。

# ⑦ まっすぐ行って下さい

■学習者の
　日本語レベル：初級

■学習者の年齢：特になし

■所 要 時 間：15分

## アクティビティのねらい

単語や文の意味を行動で表現する

### 重要な表現

● 「まっすぐ行って下さい」
● 「右／左に曲がって下さい」
● 「止まってください」

### あらかじめ必要な知識

● 場所を表す表現 (ここ、そこ、右、左、かど、信号、つきあたり、〜を、〜まで)
● 移動を表す表現 (行ってください、曲がってください、止まってください)

### 準備するもの

● アイマスクまたは手ぬぐいなど目をおおうもの
● 机を移動して、教室内に道路を作る

### 進め方

① クラス全員で道案内に必要な表現を学ぶ。
② 2人ずつペアになり、1人は目かくしをし、もう1人はその生徒の後ろに立つ。
③ 後ろの生徒は、目かくしした生徒に道案内の指示を与え、2人でスタートから
　　ゴールまでたどりつく。

### 先生方からのアドバイス

● 日本語のレベルに合わせて、指示の数を多くしていく。
● 教室内での移動が困難な場合は、小さな積み木などを使って行ってもよい。例えば、
　町 (道、信号、建物、公園などを含む) が描かれたプリントを使って、積み木など
　を人とし、プリント上で動かしてもよい。(次ページの図参照)
● 日本の道案内では、道路自体に名前が付けられていない場合が多いこと、「〜の角
　を右に〜」というような表現が多く用いられることに気づかせる。

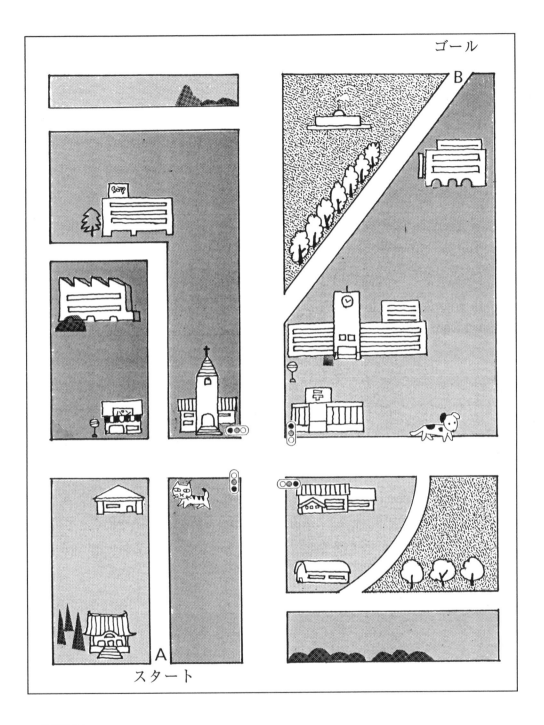

＜参考資料＞

　『生き生き日本語』福田和恵、メアリー、シスク、野口ほか著　1994年
　Iki Iki Nihongo: Live Action Japanese. Berkeley, CA: Command Performance Language Institute.

**付録**

● 地図

**箱の中身は？**

■学習者の
　日本語レベル：初級

■学習者の年齢：6才～8才

■所 要 時 間：5分

**アクティビティのねらい**

**ことばをよく聴く**

**重要な表現**

● 「箱の中にあるものは何ですか」

● 「赤いものです」「着るものです」

● 「～ です」

**あらかじめ必要な知識**

● これまでに学習した語彙

**準備するもの**

● 前面に大きく「？」をつけた小さな箱または缶

● 学習したことばの絵か文字をカードに書いたものを、1枚から5枚ぐらい箱または缶に入れておく。

　　　例：

**進め方**

① 生徒たちは、順番に、箱の中に入っているものの絵 (単語、文字) を当ててみる。前回に学習した中から選ぶなど、その範囲は、教師が決める。

② これまでに何が出てきたかよく聞いておき、順番がきたら、これまでに出ていないものを推測する。

③ 当たった場合には、箱の中からそのカードを取り出す。

**先生方からのアドバイス**

●クラスの始めや終わりの5分間を使う。

●座席順にスピーディに回し、長く考えたり、言いよどんでいる生徒は遠慮なくとばす。

●ひと回りしても答えが出ない場合には、ヒントを与える。

　　例:「着るもの」「食べ物」「赤いもの」

●前に言ったことばをよく聞いておくように、生徒に注意を促す。

●生徒によって発言の数がかたよらないように、必ず、順番通りに当てていく。

**⑨ 数ゲーム**

■学習者の
　日本語レベル：初級

■学習者の年齢：6才〜13才

■所 要 時 間：10分

## アクティビティのねらい

### 身体全体を使って楽しく数を覚える

**重要な表現**

●数の表現

**あらかじめ必要な知識**

●最低20ぐらいまでの数が数えられること

**準備するもの**

●特になし

**進め方**

① 5人〜10人のグループを作り、輪になって座る。

② 任意の連続した番号を1人ずつ割り当てる。

③ グループ全員が、4拍子のリズムで、次の動作を行う。

　　1拍目　　両手で膝をたたく。

　　2拍目　　両手をたたく。

　　3拍目　　右手の親指と中指でパチンとならす。

　　4拍目　　左手の親指と中指でパチンとならす。

④ 最初の人は、3拍目に右手の親指と中指でパチンとならしながら、自分の番号を言い、4拍目に左手の親指と中指でパチンとならしながら、グループ内で割り当てられた番号の中から自分の好きな番号を言う。

⑤ その番号に該当する人が、④をくり返す。

**先生方からのアドバイス**

●数を習いたての頃は、数を書いたカードを生徒の見える所に置いてもよい。

●手を動かしながら数を言うには、コンビネーションが必要なので、スピードは、年齢や日本語のレベルに合わせる。

●よく似た数字の発音練習にも使える。

<table>
<tr><td rowspan="3">⑩ 仲間をつくろう</td><td>■学習者の<br>　日本語レベル：初級</td></tr>
<tr><td>■学習者の年齢：6才〜10才</td></tr>
<tr><td>■所 要 時 間：10分</td></tr>
</table>

## アクティビティのねらい

ことばを聞き、理解する練習をする

**重要な表現**

●「〜ですか」

　「はい、そうです」

　「いいえ、違います」

●「〜を持っていますか」

　「はい、持っています」

　「いいえ、持っていません」

**あらかじめ必要な知識**

●数字、色、動物、形などの単語

**準備するもの**

● グループ数に相当する種類の絵カードを1グループの人数分 (例えば、3人ずつ5グループの場合には、5種類のカードを3枚ずつ用意する)

●絵カードを入れる袋

●グループの人数分の絵カードをそれぞれ重複しないように袋に入れ、セットとする

絵カードの例

**進め方**

① 各グループが同じ人数になるようにグループ分けする。

② 全てのグループに絵カード1セットを入れた袋を与える。

③ 袋から、1人ずつ絵カードを1枚取り出し、他の生徒に見せないで、胸にあてておく。

④ 教師の合図で、全員が立ち上がり、自由に動き回ってまわりの生徒に自分の持っているカードと同じものを持っているかどうかたずねる。このときの質問は、次のように決めておく。

　　例:「赤い丸ですか」/「赤い丸を持っていますか」

　　　「はい、そうです」「いいえ、違います」または「持っています」「いいえ、持っていません」

⑤ 同じカードの仲間が集まったら、すばやく座る。

**先生方からのアドバイス**

● 教師は、生徒が絵カードを見せないで、応答表現を使っているかをチェックして回る。

● 絵カードの代わりに、小さなおもちゃ (プラスチック製の野菜や果物、消しゴムの動物など) を用意してもよいが、回収が困難なこともあるので、その点を考えておくこと。

● 決められた応答表現は、あくまでも参考とし、「〜持ってる?」「うん、持って (い) る」「ううん、持って (い) ない」という会話体でもよい。

| | ■学習者の<br>　日本語レベル：初級 |
| --- | --- |
| ⑪ 今何時ですか | ■学習者の年齢：8才〜18才 |
| | ■所要時間：20分 |

**アクティビティのねらい**

時の表現を使ってみる

## 重要な表現

- ●「もしもし。そちらでは、今何時ですか」
- ●「〜では、〜時です」
- ●「世界の主な首都の名前 (カタカナで表記)」
- ●朝、昼、夕方、夜中、晩

## あらかじめ必要な知識

- ●簡単な質問のやりとり

## 準備するもの

- ●(おもちゃの) 電話器
- ●世界の時差を示した地図 (付録参照)

## 進め方

① A、Bのペアが1組になり、ロールプレイをする。A、Bの役割は生徒と一緒に決める。新聞の特派員と国内の記者、家族のメンバー同士、または、国際電話の交換手と客などいろいろな役割が考えられる。

②「もしもし。こちらAです。今〜 (首都名) では〜時ですが、そちらでは今何時ですか」

「こちらBです。〜 (首都名) では、〜時ですよ」

## 先生方からのアドバイス

- ●特に、「朝早く／夜遅くすみません」といった早朝や深夜に電話をかけたときの謝罪表現を学習することもできる。

## 付録

- ●時差を示した世界地図

**⑫ 連想ゲーム**

■学習者の
　日本語レベル：初級

■学習者の年齢：6才～13才

■所 要 時 間：15分

**アクティビティのねらい**

意味と関連づけながらことばの練習をする

**重要な表現**

●特になし

**あらかじめ必要な知識**

●特になし

**準備するもの**

●これまでに学習した単語のリストとそれを導くヒント

**進め方**

① いくつかのグループに分かれる。

② 教師が何か1つのことばを選んで、そのことばについてヒントを1つ出す。

③ 教師のヒントを聞いて、順番に教師の選んだことばを当てる。

　　例: 教師が「箸」と言う言葉で問題を出す場合

　　教　師：　　ヒント1、「長い」です

　　グループA：へび

　　グループB：ロープ

　　教　師：　　ヒント2、「食べる」です

　　グループA：にんじん

　　グループB：(お) そば

　　教　師：　　ヒント3、「2本」です

　　グループA：(お) はし

　　教　師：　　あたり！グループAの勝ち

④ 次回は、勝ったグループから始める。

**先生方からのアドバイス**

●生徒のレベルに合わせ、ヒントは、母語または英語で与えてもよい。

●ヒントは前もって用意しておき、テンポよく与える。

●テンポを速くするために、答える時間を制限し、ベルなどで知らせてもよい。

●ヒントを出す役を生徒にやらせてもよいが、テンポが落ちてしまいがちなので、注意する。

# ⓱ あいうえお並べ

■学習者の
　日本語レベル：初級

■学習者の年齢：6才〜13才

■所 要 時 間：20分

## アクティビティのねらい

五十音順と位置関係を示すことばを学習する

## 重要な表現

● 「となり (上、下、前、後、次) は何ですか」

## あらかじめ必要な知識

● ひらがなの読み

● 簡単な質疑応答

## 準備するもの

● グループの数分のひらがなカード、またはカタカナカード (五十音) のセット

## 進め方

① 5〜6人のグループに分かれる。

② カードで五十音表が並べられる程度のスペースをとり、円座する。

③ カードを各グループに配る。カードはよくシャッフルし、1カ所に伏せておく。

④ 各グループ内でじゃんけんをし、勝った人が上からカードを取り、そのカードを真ん中に出す。

⑤ 2人目以降、じゃんけんで勝った順 (または時計まわりの順) にカードを取り、五十音表の完成を目指して、すでに出ているカードのとなりに付けられるものであれば、その位置にカードを出す。もし該当しない場合は、パスしてそのカードを手元に残す。

⑥ 2回目の順番からは、自分手持ちのカードか、新たに取ったカードの中から、すでに出ているカードのとなりに付けられるものを選んで出す。

⑦ 1人3回パスできるが、4回パスになったら負け。負けた人は手持ちのすべてのカードを五十音表の該当する箇所に並べる。

⑧ 早くカードがなくなった人が勝ち。

例:

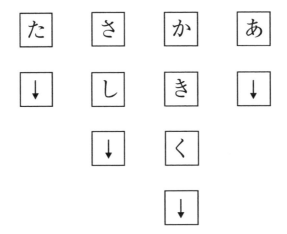

**先生方からのアドバイス**

● カードの字は大きく読みやすいように書く。

● 五十音順は、辞書を引いたり、動詞の活用を学習したりするときに役に立つ。

● 文字カードの他に助詞カード、動詞カードを作っておくと、短文作成もでき、また
　他のゲームにも使える。

**ひらがなスクラブル**

■学習者の
　日本語レベル：初級

■学習者の年齢：特になし

■所要時間：15分〜20分

**アクティビティのねらい**

意味と関連づけながらことばの練習をする

**重要な表現**

● 「ちょっと待ってください」

● 「次は、だれの番ですか」

**あらかじめ必要な知識**

● ひらがな、カタカナの読み書き

**準備するもの**

● 教師があらかじめスタートのことばを書き込んだスクラブル用紙 (正方形の数が9×9以上のマス目) (付録参照)

スタートのことばの例: 　　　げつようび

さくら

おはよう

ありがとう

**進め方**

① 2〜3人のグループに分かれる。

② 教師はスタートのことばを書き込んだスクラブル用紙を各グループに1枚ずつ配る。

③ 生徒は、順番にスタートのことばの文字を利用して、横 (左から右) 縦 (上から下) ともとなりあった1列が、全て意味のある単語になるように、スクラブル用紙上のでき上がったことばに付け加えて単語を作る。

例:

|  |  |  |  |  |  |  |
|---|---|---|---|---|---|---|
|  |  |  |  |  |  |  |
|  | あ | り | が | と | う |  |
|  |  | ん |  |  |  |  |
|  |  | ご | は | ん |  |  |
|  |  |  |  |  |  |  |

**先生方からのアドバイス**

● 日本語の書き方の規則にのっとって、下から上、右から左へは、書かせない。
● クラス全体で1つのスクラブルを行うときには、OHPを使用してもよい。

**付録**

● スクラブル用紙

| | ■学習者の<br>　日本語レベル：初級 |
|---|---|
| **15** わたし | ■学習者の年齢：6才〜13才 |
| | ■所 要 時 間：2分〜3分 |

**アクティビティのねらい**

意味と関連づけながらことばの練習をする

**重要な表現**

●わたしの顔には、穴が7つ

**あらかじめ必要な知識**

●身体の部分の名称

**準備するもの**

●特になし

**進め方**

●次の詩を、口唱しながら、指さしたり、手足を伸ばしたり、手をたたいたりする。

| ＝ ♩　　♪ ＝ ♪
⊓ ＝ ♫　　z ＝ 𝄽

わたしの　顔には　穴が　ななつ、
⊓ ⊓ ⊓ ⊓⊓ ⊓| ⊓|

円をつくって、まっすぐに立つ。または、教師が前に立って、学習者と向かい合う。教師の合図で生徒は歌詞を声に出して言う。

めに　　　ひと一つ　ふたつ
⊓ z　　♪| ♪　⊓|

「ひと一つ　ふたつ」と言いながら、目を人差し指で片目ずつ指さす。

はなに　　ひと一つ　ふたつ
⊓|　　♪| ♪　⊓|

以下同様に、鼻の穴を1つずつ指さす。

みみに　　ひと一つ　ふたつ
⊓|　　♪| ♪　⊓|

同様に、耳の穴を順に指さす。

くちに　　　ひとーつ
⌐｜　　 ⌐｜⌐ ♪

「ひとーつ」で、口を指さす。

わたしの　てあしは　よんほん
⌐｜⌐｜　⌐｜⌐｜　｜　｜

まっすぐに立つ。

てが　　　　いっぽん　　にーほん
⌐z　　　　｜　｜　　　｜　｜

うでを1本ずつ、ななめ上に伸ばす。

あしが　　　いっぽん　　にーほん
⌐｜　　　　｜　｜　　　｜　｜

同様に、足を1本ずつ横に開く。

▬

(この休符の間に、軽くジャンプして手足を元の位置
にもどし、まっすぐ立。)

わたしの　まわりに　は
⌐｜⌐｜　⌐｜⌐｜　｜　z

まえと　　うしろ
⌐｜　　　⌐｜

「まえと」の「と」のときに、からだの前方で手をたた
く。「うしろ」の「ろ」のときに、からだの後ろで手を
たたく。

うえと　　した
⌐｜　　　⌐z

頭の上に手を伸ばし、「うえと」の「と」で手をたたく。
下に手をおろし、「した」のあとで手をたたく。

みぎと　　ひだり
⌐｜　　　⌐｜

からだの右側に手をもってきて、「みぎと」の「と」で
手をたたく。からだの左側に手をもってきて、「ひだ
り」の「り」で手をたたく。

ひと一つ　　ふたつ　　みっつ　　よっつ

同様に、からだの前、後ろ、上、下

いつつ　　　むっつ　　ぜんぶで　むっつ

右、左の順にてをたたき、「ぜんぶで」で腕を大きく
回し、「むっつ」の「つ」で、胸の前で手をたたく。


**先生方からのアドバイス**

● 短時間でできるので、毎回オープニングなどに用いると効果的。身体を動かすので、
リズミカルに行うと踊りながら歌を歌うように楽しめる。

● ここでは、それぞれの語彙・文法は教えないが、音とジェスチャーにより、日本語
の調子に慣れるので、実際に語彙・文法を導入するとき、スムーズに入ることが
できる。

● 一度に全部を通すのが、長すぎると思われる場合には、「わたしのかおには…」のみ
数回行い、慣れてきたら、「わたしのてあしは…」を足す。さらに、「わたしのまわ
りには…」を付け加え、その後、最後の「ひとつ、ふたつ…」の部分を足すとよい。

**16 神経衰弱**

■学習者の
　日本語レベル：初級

■学習者の年齢：特になし

■所　要　時　間：10分〜15分

### アクティビティのねらい

意味と関連づけながらことばの練習をする

### 重要な表現
● 特になし

### あらかじめ必要な知識
● ひらがな、カタカナの読み

### 準備するもの
● 同じ単語をそれぞれひらがな、カタカナで書いた単語カード (15枚程度) を2組

### 進め方
① 5〜6人のグループに分かれる。

② 2組のカードをよくシャッフルし、伏せて机の上に並べる。

③ じゃんけんで順番を決める。

④ カードを1枚めくり、そのカードを声を出して読む。読めなかった場合には、裏返しに戻し、読めたら、2枚目もめくる。

⑤ 2枚目のカードが1枚目と合えば自分のものにし、合わなければ、裏返しに戻す。

⑥ カードをたくさん取った人が勝ち。

### 先生方からのアドバイス
● 日本語のレベルに合わせて、絵カードや漢字カードなども作り、カードの組み合わせをかえるとよい。

　　組み合わせの例：　　絵カードとひらがなカード

　　　　　　　　　　　ひらがなカードと漢字カード

　　　　　　　　　　　反対語

　　　　　　　　　　　カルタのような文の前半と後半

● 単にカードを読むだけのアクティビティにしないで、推理や考える力を働かせるものにすると楽しい。

　　例：「りんご」と「さかな」のカードが出たら、「食べ物です」と答える。

● カードはラミネート加工しておくと長く使える。また生徒に絵などを描いてもらうと楽しくいいものができる。

**ジェスチャー**

■学習者の
　日本語レベル：初級

■学習者の年齢：11才〜13才

■所 要 時 間：15分〜20分

## アクティビティのねらい

単語や文の意味を体で表現する

### 重要な表現

● 「わたしはだれでしょう」

● 「わたしは何でしょう」

● 「何をしていますか」「〜しています」

### あらかじめ必要な知識

● 単文を作ることができる

### 準備するもの

● 文 (または単語) を1枚のカードに1文 (1語) ずつ書いておく (1チームに6枚ぐらいが適当)

### 進め方

① 生徒は3人〜6人の2チームに分かれて座る。

② それぞれのチームから1人出て、カードを見て、皆に聞こえないように、先生とその内容を確認する。

③ 決められた時間内で、ジェスチャーをし、チームのメンバーはそれが何か当てていく。

④ 自分のチームのメンバーが当てれば得点となり、当たらなければ、相手のチームに答える権利が生じる。

### 先生方からのアドバイス

● カードに書いておくジェスチャーのテーマは、生徒の日本語レベルに合わせて単語もしくは文とする。単語の場合にはそのカテゴリーを家族、乗り物、動物、職業のように分け、前もって生徒に伝えておくとよい。

● 人数が多い場合には、2チーム1組として何組も作り、同時に行う。場所に余裕がなければ、2チーム1組だけが行い、残りの生徒は観客になる。

# ⑱ 「なる」の練習

■学習者の
　日本語レベル：初級 (入門、中)

■学習者の年齢：特になし

■所要時間：15分

## アクティビティのねらい

い形容詞、な形容詞の使い方と「なる」をつけた形の学習

## 重要な表現

- 「～になりました」
- 「～くなりました」

## あらかじめ必要な知識

- い形容詞、な形容詞
- 動詞の現在形と過去形

## 準備するもの

- 大きい紙1枚 (新聞紙など、クラス全員が見える大きさであれば、どんな紙でもよい)

## 進め方

① 1枚の紙を生徒に見せて、「これは紙です。1枚です」と言う。

② それを半分にちぎったり切ったりして「2枚になりました」と言う。

③ さらに半分に切って、「4枚になりました」と言う。

④ これを続け、「小さくなりました」と言う。

⑤ 小さくなったら、くしゃくしゃにして、「ゴミになりました」

⑥ ゴミをばらまいて、「きたなくなりました」

⑦ ゴミをひろって、「きれいになりました」

## 先生方からのアドバイス

- このアクティビティは、い形容詞、な形容詞の導入または、復習として使える。
- 特に、「きれいな」「有名な」は「な形容詞」であることに注意させる。
- 教師が全部の過程を言うより、途中から、生徒に表現させるようにするとよい。

# ⑲ 散歩にいこう

■学習者の
　日本語レベル：初級 (入門、中)

■学習者の年齢：特になし

■所 要 時 間：45分〜60分

## アクティビティのねらい

意味と関連づけながらことばの練習をする

**重要な表現**

●特になし

**あらかじめ必要な知識**

●ひらがな、カタカナの読み書き

**準備するもの**

●学校から外に出る許可

●記録用の用紙

●書くための台になるような硬めのフォルダー

●えんぴつ

**進め方**

① 教師と生徒とで散歩する道順を決める。

② 散歩の途中でさがすものの範囲や種類を決める。

　　例: カタカナのことば、動くもの、丸いもの、など

③ 2〜3人のグループに分かれる。

④ 散歩にでかける。

⑤ グループごとに、見つけたことばを記録していく。

⑥ 記録したことばなどをクラスで発表／掲示する。

**先生方からのアドバイス**

●住んでいる地域にある日本料理店や日本食料品店に連れていくことができれば、楽しい。

●父兄の参加を求めるとよい。

●五十音中の各音で始まることばをさがしてもよい。また、「ん」も加えて、「ん」から始まることばがないことに気づかせることもできる。(付録参照)

**付録**

●ことばさがしシート

## ㉒ 売っています、売っていません

■学習者の
　日本語レベル：初級 (入門、中)

■学習者の年齢：特になし

■所 要 時 間：15分〜45分

### アクティビティのねらい

て形の練習

**重要な表現**

● 「売って (い) ますか」

● 「はい、売って (い) ます」

● 「いいえ、売って (い) ません」

**あらかじめ必要な知識**

● 簡単な質問のやりとり

● 簡単な文の聴き取り

**準備するもの**

● 質問ワークシート (付録参照)

| 品名　店の名前 | フィルム | カメラ | ボールペン |
|---|---|---|---|
| ABCマート | | | |
| XYZマート | | | |
| 123ショップ | | | |

**進め方**

① だれでもが知っているような店やその地域で知られている店の名前を取り上げて、質問用紙に書く。

② 教師は、クラス全員を対象に、具体的に品物の名をあげ、その品がそれぞれの店で売っているかどうかたずねる。生徒は売っている場合には○、売っていない場合には×を質問用紙に記入する。

　Q 「…で〜を売っていますか」

　A 「はい、売っています」／「いいえ、売っていません。」

③ 生徒全員が記入し終わったら、4〜5人のグループに分ける。

④ 各グループで代わり番こに質問をし、答えは質問用紙の○×に応じてする。

**先生方からのアドバイス**

● 身近な語彙を増やすためにも効果的である。
● 教師は各グループに店の名や売っているものを決めさせてもよい。あとで、それら
　をグループごとに発表させてもよい。

**付録**

● 質問ワークシート

**21 袋の中は何でしょう**

■学習者の
　日本語レベル：初級 (入門、中)

■学習者の年齢：特になし

■所 要 時 間：15分〜20分

**アクティビティのねらい**

体験を通してことばを練習する

**重要な表現**

●「〜らしい」

**あらかじめ必要な知識**

●「名詞／動詞 (辞書形) ＋らしい」

**準備するもの**

●4〜5人のグループに1つの袋 (布製で口をしばることができるものがよい)

●袋の中に入れるものとして消しゴム、さいころ、スポンジ、テニスボール、紙コップなどを人数分

**進め方**

① 4〜5人のグループに分ける。各グループに物の入った袋を1つずつ配る。

② 1人ずつ袋に手を入れ、「〜 (が入っている) らしい」と言う。推量なので、間違ってもかまわない。自分のつかんだ物を覚えておく。

③ 4人で協力し、袋に入っている物を当て、それを書きとめる。

④ 書きとめたメモに従って、中に入っている物をグループごとに発表させる。

⑤ 最後に袋の中の物を取り出してメモと照合する。

**先生方からのアドバイス**

●袋の中に入れる物は、大きさ、重さ、手触りなどが似ている物がよい。

●「な形容詞＋らしい」もここで学習するとよい。

●全部当たったら、ステッカーなどのごほうびを与えてもよい。

<table>
<tr><td>■</td></tr>
</table>

**㉒ 持っています、持っていません**

■学習者の
　日本語レベル：初級 (入門、中)

■学習者の年齢：特になし

■所 要 時 間：15分

| アクティビティのねらい |
|---|
| て形の練習 |

**重要な表現**

● 「〜 (を) 持っていますか」

● 「はい、持っています」

● 「いいえ、持っていません」

**あらかじめ必要な知識**

● 簡単な質問のやりとり

● 簡単な文の聴き取り

**準備するもの**

● 質問ワークシート

例:

| 名 前 ＼ 品 名 | ファミコン | ビデオ | 千円札 |
|---|---|---|---|
| ローラ | | | |
| トム | | | |
| ジョニー | | | |

**進め方**

① 最初は先生対全クラスで練習する。

　Q 「〜さん、ファミコンを持っていますか」

　A 「はい、持っています」／「いいえ、持っていません」

② 先生が質問をし、当たった生徒は答える。他の生徒はそれを聞きながら、質問ワークシートに〇、×で記入していく。

③ 次に最低3人 (聞く人、答える人、記録する人) のグループに分かれて練習する。

④ 各グループで聞きたい項目を考え、同じ要領で質問をする。

⑤ 最後に質問ワークシートをまとめ、クラスで発表する。

例: 〜さんは、＿＿＿を持っています。

　　　＿＿＿は、2人の人が持っています。

**先生方からのアドバイス**

● 「あります」「持っています」の違いについてよく質問が出るので、その違いを説明する。

● 所持品については、定期、印鑑、貯金通帳、お金、友達の写真、まんが、パスポートなどいろいろ聞くことができる。プライバシーの侵害にならない程度に項目を作るとよい。

● 初めは、品物の数を少なくした方がよい。

**付録**

● 質問ワークシート

# ㉓ 違うものなあに

## アクティビティのねらい

これまで習った語彙の意味をまとめ、同時に集中して聴く力を養う

## 重要な表現

● 「よく聞いてください。この中で、違っているのはどれですか。1つ選んでください」

## あらかじめ必要な知識

● これまでに学習した語彙

## 準備するもの

● これまでに学習した語彙の中から、1つだけ種類の違うものを入れた4つ1組の単語を10組。

　　例：りんご、いぬ、バナナ、いちご

　　　　この場合、「いぬ」が正解。他はすべて果物だから。

## 進め方

　① 教師はまずクラス全体に「よく聞いてください。この中で違っているのはどれですか。1つ選んでください」と言う。

　② 教師、または生徒の1人が、4つの単語を読み上げる。

　③ 違っているものがわかった生徒は手をあげて答える。

　④ それを選んだ理由を述べる (日本語で説明できなければ、英語または母語でもよい)。

## 先生方からのアドバイス

● 読むスピードに留意すること。なるべく自然なスピードで読みたいが、難しいものは少しゆっくり読む。

● 気分転換に、学習項目以外のことばも取り入れると楽しい。

　　例：おすし、チャーハン、天ぷら、うどん

● 日本語のレベルに合わせて、教師または生徒が種類の違うものを選び、それはなぜかを説明するアクティビティにしてもよい。例えば上の例で「うどん」を選ぶと、説明としては、「スープ／汁に入っているから」などとなる。

| ㉔ | 知っています、知りません | ■学習者の<br>　日本語レベル：初級 (入門、中)<br><br>■学習者の年齢：特になし<br><br>■所 要 時 間：15分 |
|---|---|---|

| アクティビティのねらい |
|---|
| て形の練習 |

**重要な表現**

● 「〜を知っていますか」

● 「はい、知っています」

● 「いいえ、知りません」

**あらかじめ必要な知識**

● 簡単な質問のやりとり

● 簡単な文の聴き取り

**準備するもの**

● 質問ワークシート

　　例:

| 名前　　＼　　項目 | 先生の電話番号 | ビルのくつのサイズ | レインさんの住所 |
|---|---|---|---|
| ナオミ | | | |
| デイビッド | | | |
| ポーラ | | | |

**進め方**

① 先生対クラス全員で練習する。

② 教師は生徒を指名し質問をする。指名された生徒は答える。

　　Q　「先生の電話番号を知っていますか」

　　A　「はい、知っています」／「いいえ、知りません」

③ 他の生徒はそれを聞きながら、質問ワークシートに〇、×で記入していく。

④ 4〜5人のグループに分かれる。

⑤ 教師の代わりに生徒の1人が質問し、グループ内で②を行う。質問ワークシートに質問のやりとりを書き込む。

**先生方からのアドバイス**

● 「知っていません」ではなく、「知りません」であることに注意する。

● 〜 (さん) の誕生日、〜 (さん) の趣味、有名人の飼っている猫の名前など楽しい質問項目を考える。

● 質問項目は名詞だけでなく、「〜 (さん) がいつアメリカに行くのか知っていますか」「〜 (さん) が何時に起きたか知っていますか」などのように文章にしてもよい。

**付録**

● 質問ワークシート

| **25** クロスワード | ■学習者の<br>　日本語レベル：初級 (入門、中) |
| --- | --- |
| | ■学習者の年齢：特になし |
| | ■所 要 時 間：20分 |

**アクティビティのねらい**

意味と関連づけながらことばの練習をする

**重要な表現**
- 特になし

**あらかじめ必要な知識**
- これまでに学習したことばの読み

**準備するもの**
- クロスワード用紙1枚と、メモ用紙または解答用紙1枚

**進め方**

① クロスワードのトピックが何であるか、いくつの単語が隠されているかを生徒に示す。

　トピックの例:「家族のよびかた」「乗りもの」

② 生徒は「始め」の合図で単語を探し、見つけた単語を線で囲む。

**先生方からのアドバイス**
- 日本語のレベルに合わせて、英語 (または母語) でヒントの書いてある日本語の単語などを一緒に読むことをしてもよい。

　例: いぬ—man's best friend
- 書く訓練をさせる場合は、生徒に見つけたことばを別紙に書き出させてもよい。
- 低学年や、文字を習いたての頃は、ことばを黒板に書いておいてもよい。

**付録**
- 「あいさつのことば」(クロスワード用紙と解答)
- 「教室にあるもの」(クロスワード用紙と解答)
- 「えとの動物」(クロスワード用紙と解答)

<table>
<tr><td rowspan="2">**26** **ルーレット**</td><td>■学習者の<br>　日本語レベル：初級 (入門、中)</td></tr>
<tr><td>■学習者の年齢：6才～10才<br><br>■所 要 時 間：10分～15分</td></tr>
</table>

**アクティビティのねらい**

数字やことばのつなぎ方を学ぶ

**重要な表現**
- 数の数え方 (例: ～こ、～本、～枚)
- 数や色の表現と名詞のつなぎ方

**あらかじめ必要な知識**
- 数字、色の名前
- かな (学習者のレベルによっては、漢字) の読み

**準備するもの**
- 1枚に1つずつ物の名前を書いた人数分以上の枚数のカード
- ルーレット板2枚 (Iに数字、IIに色を書いておく) (付録参照)

**進め方**
① 3～4人のグループに分かれる。
② 中央にルーレットを置き、各グループで床に円座するか、丸いテーブルを囲んで腰かける。
③ カードは山にしておき、生徒に1枚のカードを取らせる。
④ 生徒間で順番を決め、2つのルーレットの矢印を回す。
⑤ 矢印が止まったところの数と色、そしてカードのことばをつなぐ。

例:

1＋しろい＋ ほん ／3＋あかい＋ えんぴつ

⑥ 適当な数え方をつないで言う。
例: 1さつの白い本／3本の赤いえんぴつ
または、
白い本1さつ／赤いえんぴつ3本

**先生方からのアドバイス**

●ルーレット板は教師が手作りするか、生徒に作らせる。

●レベルによっては、簡単な漢字を表現に加えてもよい。


**付録**

●ルーレット板Ⅰ(数字)

●ルーレット板Ⅱ(色)

■学習者の
　日本語レベル：初級 (入門、中)

■学習者の年齢：特になし

■所 要 時 間：10分～15分

## アクティビティのねらい

身体の部分の名称を楽しく学習する

**重要な表現**

- 「もっと、右 (左、上、下) へ」
- 目、耳、鼻、口、まゆ

**あらかじめ必要な知識**

- 特になし

**準備するもの**

- 福笑いの顔／目、鼻、口などのない似顔絵 (画用紙ぐらいの大きさがよい) (付録参照)
- 目、鼻、口、まゆ毛など福笑いの顔／似顔絵にのせる顔の一部分 (付録参照)
- アイマスクなど目をおおうもの

**進め方**

① 4～5人のグループに分かれる。

② じゃんけんで順番を決める。

③ まず、アイマスクなどで目隠しをし、顔の一部分 (例: 目) を手に持って、それを手探りで福笑いの顔／似顔絵の上に置いていく。

④ 他の人は、「もっと右へ」などと言って助ける。

**先生方からのアドバイス**

- 年齢に合わせて、話題になっている人、お話の登場人物などの顔の似顔絵を作ると楽しい。
- 似顔絵は、新聞や雑誌のまんがを拡大したものなどを利用することができる。
- 福笑い (付録) を使う場合には、「福笑い」や「おかめ」「ひょっとこ」の由来や習慣など、文化的な説明を加えるとよい。

**付録**

- 福笑い (おかめとひょっとこ)

**アイスクリーム屋さん**

■学習者の
　日本語レベル：初級 (中、上)

■学習者の年齢：6才〜10才

■所 要 時 間：30分

### アクティビティのねらい

「アイスクリームを買う」ことを通して、
コンテストに合った単語や表現の使い方を学ぶ

**重要な表現**

- ●「これは何ですか」
- ●「バニラ／チョコレート／ストロベリーです」
- ●「コーンですか、カップですか」
- ●「シングルですか、ダブルですか」
- ●「〜 (つ) ください」
- ●「いくらですか」

**あらかじめ必要な知識**

- ●最小限の買い物の表現

**準備するもの**

- ●アイスクリーム屋さんの帽子
- ●アイスクリームの絵、またはアイスクリームのコーンを作る紙 (扇形) かカップを作る紙 (正方形)、および3色 (フレーバーの数分の色) のやわらかい紙
- ●おもちゃのお金 (日本円)

**進め方**

① アイスクリームを買う場合に必要な買い物の表現、フレーバーの種類、値段などをクラス全員で話し合い、練習する。

② アイスクリームを作る。

コーン：扇形の紙を図のようにし、紙の両端をのりづけするか、テープで止め円錐形にしたら、フレーバー用の紙を丸めて中に入れる。

カップ：正方形の紙をa〜fのように折り、カップができたら両端から押して口を開かせ、丸めたフレーバーを入れる。

**コーン**

120

## カップ

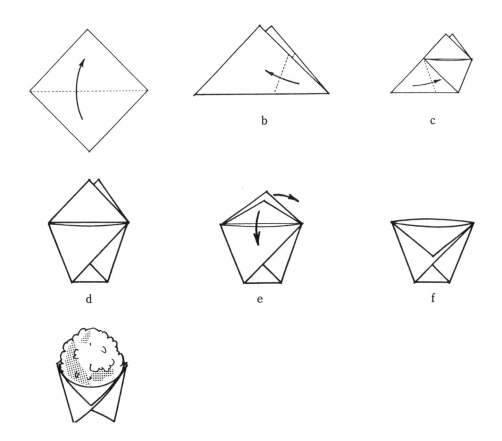

b

c

d

e

f

③ アイスクリーム屋さんの店員と客の役割を決め、ロールプレイをする。5〜6人の小グループを作り、何組かで同時にするとよい。

### 先生方からのアドバイス

● 生徒の年齢と日本語のレベルに合わせて、フレーバーは例えば3種類ぐらいをあらかじめ選んでおくとやりやすい。一般のアイスクリーム屋さんにあるフレーバーの種類を使ってもよい。

● 日本語のレベルに合わせて、自分のほしいフレーバーがない場合や、また手持ちのお金を制限し、何人分買わなければならない場合などの状況を作って、どのように対処するかを学習してもよい。

## 29 何のグループ

■学習者の
　日本語レベル：初級 (中、上)

■学習者の年齢：14才～18才

■所 要 時 間：30分

### アクティビティのねらい

動詞のグループ分けを推測することにより、動詞活用のルールを学ぶ

### 重要な表現

● 「何のグループですか」

● 「～は何形ですか」

### あらかじめ必要な知識

● 動詞のいくつかの活用形 (例: 辞書形、ます形、て形)

### 準備するもの

● これまでに学習した動詞の辞書形を書いたカード (5cm×10cm) を30枚

　 (「する」と「くる」は含めない)

### 進め方

① 3～4人のグループに分かれる。

② 各グループに30枚の動詞カードを1セットずつ配る。

③ 教師の指示した活用形に従い、動詞カードをu-動詞 (u-verb)、ru-動詞 (ru-verb) の2つのグループに分ける。

④ 新しい動詞を導入し、どちらのグループに属するか、推理してみる。

### 先生方からのアドバイス

● この時点で、u-動詞、ru-動詞を導入してもよい。

● 動詞カードは教師が準備してもいいし、各グループで生徒が書いてもよい。

● このアクティビティで既習の動詞を別の角度から検討することが、後に可能形や意向形を学ぶときに役立つ。

**数字すごろく**

■学習者の
　日本語レベル：初級 (中、上)

■学習者の年齢：6才〜10才

■所 要 時 間：15分〜20分

### アクティビティのねらい

これまで学習した単語を使って文章を作る

**重要な表現**
- 「〜さんの番です」

**あらかじめ必要な知識**
- 簡単な応答文やものの名前

**準備するもの**
- 各マスに番号の入った数字すごろく

    すごろく盤の例:

- さいころ1つ
- 参加者の人数分のコマ (各自自分のものがどれか見分けられるようにする)
- すごろくの番号分の質問カード

**進め方**
　① 4〜5人のグループに分かれて、すごろくのまわりに車座になる。

　②「ふりだし」にチップを置き、じゃんけんなどで順番を決める。

　③ 順番にさいころを振り、出た目の数だけ進み、そのマスに書かれた番号の質問カードを読む。

　　例:「この部屋にあるものを4つ言ってください」

　　　「八百屋さんにあるものを5つ言ってください」

　　　「今日のお天気はどうですか」

④ 質問カードに答えることができたら、そのマスにチップを置くことができる。答えられなかったら、カードの指示に従う。

　　カードの指示例: 犬 (猫) の鳴き声を日本語で言う。

　　「ふりだし」に戻る。

　　1回休み。

　　教室の中をスキップで1周する。

　　となりの人とじゃんけんをして勝ったら、3コマ進み、負けたら3コマ戻る。

　　日本語で早口ことばを言う。

⑤ 早く「あがり」に着いた人が勝ち。

**先生方からのアドバイス**

● 10人以内のクラスならクラス全体ですることもできるし、何人かのグループで机を寄せてグループごとに行ってもよい。

● バリエーションとして、生徒たちにすごろくを自由に作らせてもよい。ただし、その場合には、質問カードを使わずにすごろく盤上の指示に従って自由に遊ばせ、その中から楽しみながら日本語を使用させることをねらいとする。(生徒の作ったすごろく参照)

　　　　　例: 生徒の作ったすごろく

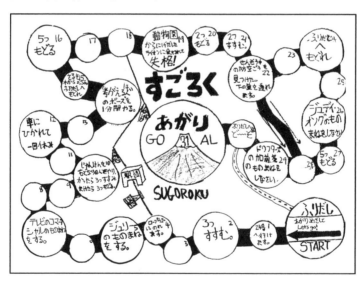

**付録**

● すごろくシート

**(31) 助詞すごろく**

## アクティビティのねらい

助詞を使って文章を作る

**重要な表現**

●「〜さんの番です」

**あらかじめ必要な知識**

●基本的な助詞の使い方

**準備するもの**

●助詞がマスに書かれたすごろく

●さいころ1つ

●参加者の人数分のコマ (各自自分のものがどれか見分けられるようにする)

**進め方**

① 4〜5人のグループに分かれて、すごろくのまわりに車座になる。

②「ふりだし」にチップを置き、じゃんけんなどで順番を決めて、最初の人がさいころを振る。

③ さいころの目の数だけ進み、そのマスに書かれた助詞を使って文を作る。

④ 正しく言えたら、そこにチップを置き、正しく言えなかったら進めず、元の位置に留まる。

⑤ 早く「あがり」に着いた人が勝ち。

**先生方からのアドバイス**

●1つの助詞にいろいろな使い方があることに、気づかせる。

**付録**

●助詞すごろくシート

<table>
<tr>
<td rowspan="2">**32** **〜とき、〜たら**</td>
<td>■学習者の<br>　日本語レベル：初級 (中、上)</td>
</tr>
<tr>
<td>■学習者の年齢：11才〜18才<br><br>■所 要 時 間：30分</td>
</tr>
</table>

| アクティビティのねらい |
|---|
| 「〜とき」「〜たら」を実際に使う |

**重要な表現**
- ●「〜とき」
- ●「〜たら」
- ●「誰でしょう」

**あらかじめ必要な知識**
- ●文レベルの発話能力

**準備するもの**
- ●人数分のワークシート

例:

なまえ: _____

1. こどものとき、_____。
   名詞

2. 頭が痛いとき、_____。
   形容詞

3. ひまなとき、_____。
   形容詞

4. がっこうにくるとき、_____。
   辞書形

5. しゅくだいをわすれたとき、_____。
   た形

6. _____とき、_____。


なまえ: _____

1. しゅくだいをわすれたら、_____。

2. 1万円をひろったら、_____。

3. 大きくなったら、_____。

4. 日本にしょうたいされたら、_____。

5. 21せいきになったら、_____。

## 進め方

① ワークシートを1枚ずつ生徒に配る。

② 生徒は、ワークシートのそれぞれの書き出しに書き加えて文を完成させる。

③ 所定の時間がきたらそれを集めて、教師か生徒が1枚ずつ読み、クラスでだれが書いたものかを当てる。

## 先生方からのアドバイス

● 人数が多い方が面白い。

## ㉝ わたしのデパート

■学習者の
　日本語レベル：初級 (中、上)

■学習者の年齢：8才〜13才

■所　要　時　間：30分

### アクティビティのねらい

ことばの意味を関連づけながら練習する

### 重要な表現

● 「〜はどこにありますか」、「〜は何階にありますか」
● 「〜は〜階にあります」
● 地下1階、1階、2階、3階、4階、5階、6階、7階、8階、屋上

### あらかじめ必要な知識

● デパートで売られている品物の名前

### 準備するもの

● デパートの絵 I (付録参照)、デパートの絵 II (付録参照)

### 進め方

① デパートの絵Iをクラス全員で学習する。
② 各自自分がほしいものを記録し、買い物リストを作る。
③ デパートの案内係役、客役を決める。
④ 客は自分の買い物リストを見て、案内係に、「〜は何階にありますか」と聞く。
⑤ 案内係は、「〜は何階にあります」と答える。
⑥ 自分のデパートの絵に、何階で何を買うかを書き込んでいき、買い物のプランを完了する。

### 先生方からのアドバイス

● 日本のデパートは、売り場構成と各階の商品の配置がほぼ決まっているので、その例を学習する。
● デパートに通常置いていないものは何か、学習者の出身地のデパートとはどの点が違っているか、それはなぜかを考え、文化の比較をしても楽しい。
● デパートの案内係は、通常「〜は3階にございます」あるいは「〜は3階婦人服売場にございます」といったていねいな表現を用いることを教えてもよい。

### 付録

● デパートの絵 I (各階の商品)、デパートの絵 II (書き込み用ブランクシート)

**作文カードゲーム**

■学習者の
　日本語レベル：初級 (中、上)

■学習者の年齢：特になし

■所 要 時 間：15分

---

**アクティビティのねらい**

助詞の復習
単文を作る

---

**重要な表現**

●いつ、どこで、だれが、何を、します

**あらかじめ必要な知識**

●「いつ、どこで、だれが、何を、します」といった形の文レベルの読み書き

**準備するもの**

●トランプ程度の大きさの白紙のカード (生徒1人につき5枚)

**進め方**

① 教師は黒板に次のように書いておく。

　1. だれが　2. いつ　3. どこで　4. 何を　5. します

② 生徒に1人5枚ずつ、カードを配る。

③ 生徒はカードに1から5の番号を書き、それぞれのカードに番号に該当する内容のことばを書いて5枚で文になるようにする。

④ 1から5のカードを番号別に集めてシャッフルする。

⑤ 読み手を5人選び、1から5のカードを割り当てる。

⑥ 読み手は集めたカードを番号順に読む。

**先生方からのアドバイス**

●1クラス15人以内だと、このアクティビティは効果的である。

●もともと生徒の書いた文が平凡なものであっても、シャッフルの結果偶然できた文は面白くなる。笑っているなかで、文の構造、助詞の使い方が確認できればよい。どの文が一番面白かったかを最後に話し合うこともできる。

●応用とし1〜5の他に「だれと」をつけ加えてカードを6枚にしてもよい。

例:　　1　　　2　　　　3　　　　4　　　　5　　　　　6

　　｜毎日｜プールで｜マイクが｜ねこと｜しゅくだいを｜します。｜

●カードの順を入れ換えて読み上げさせ、語順がかなり自由に動かせるという日本語の特徴を意識させるとよい。

| **35** どの人でしょう | ■学習者の<br>日本語レベル：初級 (中、上)、<br>中級 |
| | ■学習者の年齢：特になし |
| | ■所要時間：20分 |

## アクティビティのねらい

ことばと意味を関連づけながら練習する

**重要な表現**

- 「背が高い／低いです」
- 「太って／やせています」
- 「めがねをかけています／いません」
- 「髪が茶色／黒です」
- 「笑っています」
- 「この人です」
- 「右から〜人 (目) ／番目の人です」

**あらかじめ必要な知識**

- 身体的な特徴の描写

**準備するもの**

- 生徒の持ってくる家族の写真や、団体写真など

**進め方**

① 1枚の写真を一緒に見ることができるぐらいの人数のグループに分かれる。

② 各グループで写真に写っている人物の特徴を述べる人を選ぶ。

③ 選ばれた人は、グループに写真を見せながら、写真の中の特定の人物について、身体的な特徴を3つから5つ述べる。

④ グループの他の人は該当する人がだれかを当てる。

**先生方からのアドバイス**

- 日本語のレベルに合わせて、句や文章で人物の特徴を述べる。
- 家族の集合写真など、生徒の持ってきた写真を使って、写っている人たちの趣味、職業、顔の表情、着ている服などについて述べれば、表現の幅が広がる。
- 日本人同士では、目の色や髪の色は、特徴とならないことが多い。人物を描写する際、どのような表現が使われるのか、「行方不明者」の掲示や迷子のお知らせなどの表現を集めて話し合うとよい。

**36** 文を作りましょう

アクティビティのねらい

動詞の活用形を学ぶ

**重要な表現**
- 特になし

**あらかじめ必要な知識**
- 動詞の活用

**準備するもの**
- 問題用の文章 (動詞の部分をブランクにしたもの)

**進め方**
① 動詞の活用形を選びあらかじめ指定する。

例:「きょうは、ます形 (た形、辞書形) を使いましょう」

② 3人ずつのグループに分ける。

③ 各グループの1人が、教師の所へ行き、問題の文をもらう。問題の文は、動詞が抜けている。

例: トム君は算数を＿＿＿＿＿＿

④ 問題の文をもらった生徒は、その文をグループの他の2人に口頭で伝える。

⑤ 2人は適当な動詞を考え、それぞれが紙に答えを書く。

⑥ 教師の合図で同時にその答えをみんなに見せる。

**先生方からのアドバイス**
- グループ間の競争にしてもよい。例えば、2人が同じ答えを書いたらそのグループの得点とし、正しい答えでも2人の答えが同じでなければ得点にならないなどのルールを考え、ゲーム形式にすると、日本語の能力に関係のないところでも点が取れ、劣等感を感じることなくゲームを楽しむことができる。

**(37) 見えますか?**

■学習者の
　日本語レベル：初級 (中、上)

■学習者の年齢：8才～18才

■所要時間：20分～45分

**アクティビティのねらい**

意味と関連づけながらことばの練習をする

### 重要な表現

● 「どこがあいていますか」
　　上、下、右、左、ななめ上　ななめ下

● 「これは何ですか」
● 「これを読んでください」「読めません」(ひらがな、カタカナの視力表を使ったとき)

### あらかじめ必要な知識

● 位置の表現
● ひらがな、カタカナの読み
● 動詞の (可能) 否定形の表現

### 準備するもの

● 視力表 (付録参照)
● 視力検査表 (付録参照)
● ポインター (棒やものさしなど)
● 片目を隠すもの (しゃもじやスプーンのようなもの)

### 進め方

① 拡大した視力表を黒板やイーゼルに貼る。
② 生徒は3人ずつのグループに分かれる。
③ 各グループで視力検査をしてもらう人、検査する人 (検査係) 、記録する人 (記録係) を決める。
④ 検査する人は、「これは何ですか」「これを読んでください」とポインターで示しながら、聞いていく。
⑤ 検査係と記録係が表のどこまで読めたかを確認し、その人の視力を決める。
⑥ 記録係が視力を書き込み、検査を受けた人に報告する。
⑦ 個人の視力表の観察欄に、「よく見えます」「よく読めます」「たいへんよくできました」などのコメントを入れる。

**先生方からのアドバイス**

● 一度に3人から多くて4〜5人しかできないので、全員参加できるようにそれ相応の数のセットを用意するか、または1セットで行い、他の生徒は見ている、という形にしてもよい。

● 漢字を使用した視力表を作り練習に使ってもよい。その場合は下 (視力のいい方) にいくほど、画数の多い字、もしくは難しい字を配置してもよい。

**付録**

●視力表

●視力検査表

**38 メニュー作り**

■学習者の
　日本語レベル：初級 (上)

■学習者の年齢：8才〜10才

■所 要 時 間：20分

**アクティビティのねらい**

メニューを作り、それを使ってロールプレイをすることで、
レストランで使う表現を身につける

### 重要な表現

● ひとつ、1本、一人前、定食、飲み物

### あらかじめ必要な知識

● 料理や飲み物の書き表し方

● 日本料理など、料理の種類と名称

● 料理や飲み物のおよその値段

### 準備するもの

● メニューを作るための硬めの用紙 (色紙など)

### 進め方

① 5〜6人ずつのグループに分かれる。

② 店の種類を決める(ファーストフード、和食、中華料理、イタリア料理、タイ料理など)。

③ 店の名前、メニュー、値段を決める。各グループがいろいろな種類のメニューを選択する。

④ メニューを作成する (少し大きめに書くとよい)。

⑤ このメニューを使って、2人〜4人ぐらいの友人や家族が店に食事に行くという設定でロールプレイをする。

### 先生方からのアドバイス

● メニュー作成はコンピュータを使用すると幅の広いものができる。

● 自分のまわりにあるメニューや、日本語のメニューの実物が入手できればクラスで紹介するとよい。OHP などで紹介したり、回覧したりして、参考として使う。メニューの実物を使って、次のような質問もできる。

「4人家族が7000円の予算で外食をしたいと思います。あなたなら、何を注文しますか」

「日本と〜との食事の値段を比べてみましょう」

「〜 (国名または〜さんの国) では食べる前に／食べた後に何か言いますか」

● ロールプレイをする場合、キーワードは次のようなものである。

「いらっしゃいませ」「いただきます」「ごちそうさまでした」「お水／おひや（おはし、おしぼり、ナイフ、フォーク、おしょうゆ、ソース) をください」

# 39 紙スライド

## アクティビティのねらい

### 時間の流れにそった文章の構成を理解し、話を作る

**重要な表現**

● 〜時〜分

● 初めに／まず、次に／そして、最後に／やがて

● ある日、そして、ところが、そこで

**あらかじめ必要な知識**

● 単文を書くこと

**準備するもの**

● 紙スライド作成用の用紙 (多少厚めのもの)

**進め方**

① クラス全員に用意した紙スライドを見せる。

② 生徒は4〜5人のグループに分かれる。

③ 4コマの絵とお話をグループで作る。

④ 紙スライドを作る。

⑤ 紙スライドが完成したら、クラスで発表する。

⑥ 発表したお話を文章として書く。

**先生方からのアドバイス**

● 紙スライドの作成に時間がかかるが、一度作っておけば、何回も使用できる。時の流れを明確に説明し、把握できるよい教材となる。

時間の流れにそって作るお話の例:

例1:

太郎君がうまれました。

幼稚園生になりました。

小学生になりました。

中学生になりました。

例2:

なんの卵でしょう。

音がします。象かな。かいじゅうかな。

ことこと動いています。象かな。

あっ、割れた。ひよこが出てきた。

例3:

| | |
|---|---|
| 7: 00 | 起きます。 |
| 7: 05 | さあ、朝ごはんですよ。 |
| 7: 15 | そして、歯磨きをします。 |
| 7: 45 | 行ってきます。 |

紙スライドの例:

 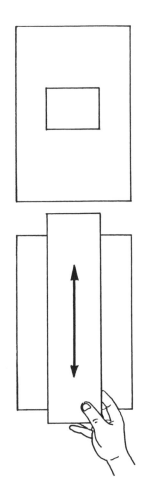

**40 ～曜日はどうですか**

■学習者の
　日本語レベル：初級 (上)、中級
■学習者の年齢：中学、高校
　　　　　　　　レベル
■所要時間：20分

**アクティビティのねらい**

相手と交渉し、時間などを決める

**重要な表現**

● 「～ませんか」(勧誘)

● 「～曜日 (日、時) はどうですか」

● 「いいですね」

● 「ちょっとだめです」

● 「～曜日、 (日、時) にしましょう」

**あらかじめ必要な知識**

● 時間の表現 (曜日、日、時間)

● 週末にすることや行く場所についての表現

　　例: ボーリング、映画、ハンバーガー・ショップ

**準備するもの**

● 人数分のスケジュール表 (付録参照)

**進め方**

　① 2人でペアを組む。

　② 1人1枚、スケジュール表を配る。

　③ 教師が課題を出す。

　④ 2人が交渉しながら、約束の日や時間を決める。

　⑤ 決定したスケジュールを発表する。

**先生方からのアドバイス**

● 初級レベルの生徒では、教師があらかじめスケジュール表にスケジュールを書きこんでおくとよい。

● 生徒のレベルににに応じて、より複雑な課題を出すこともできる。

　　例1:　生徒会がダンスパーティを計画している。学校の暦を検討しながら、パーティの日、準備委員会開催の日などを決める。

　　例2:　友達同士で映画を見に行く計画をしたい。

● 日本語のレベルに合わせて、目上の人と交渉する場合、相手の提案したスケジュールが都合悪い場合、電話で交渉する場合などの表現を学習するとよい。

**付録**
● スケジュール表

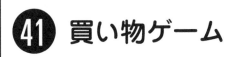

**41** 買い物ゲーム

■学習者の
　日本語レベル：初級 (上)、中級

■学習者の年齢：6才〜13才

■所 要 時 間：15分〜20分

### アクティビティのねらい

買い物のしかたをロールプレイで経験してみる

**重要な表現**

● 「いらっしゃいませ」

● 「(〜は〜で) いくらですか」

● 「(〜で) 〜円です」

● 「毎度ありがとうございます」

**あらかじめ必要な知識**

● 買い物をするときに使う表現

**準備するもの**

● 品目の絵を描いたカード

　　例: 八百屋さんなら、なす、きゅうりなど野菜の絵を描いたもの

● 買い物をしたカードを入れる大きな袋、またはかご

● (おもちゃの) お金 (日本円)

● 値段カード

**進め方**

　① 5〜6人のグループに分かれる。

　② グループごとに店員と客の役割を決める。

　③ 店員役の生徒は、品物の絵カードを並べ、それぞれの品物の値段を決めて、
　　 値段カードを品物の前に並べる。

　④ ロールプレイで客が買い物をする。

**先生方からのアドバイス**

● 絵カードの代わりに、プラスチックの模型などを使ってもよい。

| ■学習者の<br>日本語レベル：すべてのレベル |
| --- |
| ■学習者の年齢：特になし |
| ■所要時間：20分〜40分 |

| アクティビティのねらい |
| --- |
| 単語や文字を楽しく覚える |

### 重要な表現
- 「できました」
- 「たて」、「よこ」、「ななめ」、「コの字型」、「×型」

### あらかじめ必要な知識
- 文字の読み (ひらがな、カタカナ、漢字の中で、そのときの学習項目を使用)

### 準備するもの
- 人数分のビンゴ用紙（一枚一枚が違う文字配列になっている）
- 読み札
- チップ (置き札。「おはじき」や「豆」のようなものでもよい)

### 進め方
① チップを置く形を決める。

　例: バツ (×)型／たて／よこ／ななめ／コの字型など

② 読み札を箱などに入れて、見えなくしておく。

③ 読み札の読み手（先生または生徒）は箱の中を見ずにカードを引き、読み上げる。

④ 生徒は、読み手が読んだところに、チップを置く。

⑤ 決められた形に全部チップがのった生徒は、「できました」と言う。

### 先生方からのアドバイス
- ビンゴ用紙を作るのに時間がかかるが、一度作っておけば、何回も使える。特に、用紙の素材を選べば長く使える。
- レベルによって、いろいろな種類のビンゴが考えられる。
　例:　ひらがなビンゴ、カタカナビンゴ、漢字ビンゴ (漢数字／日本人の名前／地名など)
　　　トピックビンゴ (家族関係／教室の名前／学習科目／食べ物の名前など)

例1:

| で | き | ま | し | た |
|---|---|---|---|---|
| ね | に | さ | う | て |
| ち | か | そ | た | く |
| あ | す | け | こ | な |
| の | し | つ | い | せ |
| え | し | き | ぬ | お |

例2:

| で | き | ま | し | た |
|---|---|---|---|---|
| すいか | にく | かさ | いぬ | おの |
| たいこ | なに | くち | ねこ | おに |
| とけい | て | ✕ | いえ | うそ |
| ちかい | しか | かき | そこ | あさ |
| けいと | なし | つき | うえ | あせ |

例3:

| で | き | ま | し | た |
|---|---|---|---|---|
| ニャー | シャー | ティン | ション | ビュッ |
| チャッ | ピュー | ジョン | リュー | シュー |
| フェア | ジェ | キャッ | フォー | チョ |
| ディー | ショー | ニュー | シュッ | リュッ |
| キャー | フィン | チュー | ミュー | チョッ |

例4:

| で | き | ま | し | た |
|---|---|---|---|---|
| 三十九 | 七 | 三十五 | 七十 | 一 |
| 十四 | 四十八 | 九十一 | 二十六 | 五十二 |
| 六十二 | 三十一 | ✕ | 六十三 | 八十七 |
| 八十六 | 七十七 | 九十九 | 三十八 | 二十五 |
| 十三 | 四十 | 三十一 | 七十九 | 五十三 |

**間違いはどこ？**

■学習者の
　日本語レベル：すべてのレベル

■学習者の年齢：特になし

■所要時間：5分～10分

### アクティビティのねらい

間違っている単語などに焦点をおくことで、授業の導入とする

**重要な表現**

●特になし

**あらかじめ必要な知識**

●特になし

**準備するもの**

●すでに学習した、単語、文章、文型の正しい表記、アクセント、イントネーション、文法などの中からポイントを選んでおくこと

●黒板に間違いを含む単語、文章などを書いておくこと

　　　例：えんぱつ

　　　　　わたしわいぬをすちです。

　　　　　エリザベスを見れば、知らせてください。

**進め方**

　① 生徒は教室に入ると同時に　黒板に書かれた単語または文の間違いを見つけ、正しいものをノートに書く。

　　　例：えんぴつ

　　　　　わたしはいぬがすきです。

　　　　　エリザベスを見たら、知らせてください。

　② 全員がそろったところで、答え合わせをする。

**先生方からのアドバイス**

●初期の段階では、いくつ間違いがあるかを教えておいた方がよい。

●初期の段階では、ポイントを1つにしぼった方がよい。

　　　例：助詞について3から4題。

　　　　　いぬ<u>で</u>すきです。

　　　　　すいか<u>に</u>たべます。

　　　　　水<u>へ</u>のみたい。

●取り上げる間違いの例は、生徒の書いたもの、言ったものから選んでおくとよい。

● アクセント、イントネーションの指導にも使える。その場合は、教師がアクセントやイントネーションの間違いを含んだ単文や単語、句などを読み、生徒に訂正させる (下線は高アクセントを示す)。

　　例: (誤)　わた<u>し</u>は　<u>い</u>ぬが　<u>す</u>きです。

　　　　(正)　わた<u>しは</u>　い<u>ぬ</u>が　すきです。

**魔法のことば**

■ 学習者の
　日本語レベル：すべてのレベル

■ 学習者の年齢：特になし

■ 所 要 時 間：特になし

**アクティビティのねらい**

日本語を話すことを奨励する

**重要な表現**

● 特になし

**あらかじめ必要な知識**

● 特になし

**準備するもの**

● 特になし

**進め方**

① 教師が「日本語です」と言い、全員で手をたたく。こうすると魔法がかかって日本語しか話せなくなる。

② 教師が「～語 (母語) です」と言い、全員で手をたたくと、魔法が解けて、～語 (母語) が話せるようになる。

**先生方からのアドバイス**

● なるべく日本語を使うようにするための一方法でもあり、また～語 (母語) が氾濫するのを防ぐことができる。

● 目標は、授業の始めから終わりまで、魔法のかかった状態でいることである。

● この魔法をかけたり、解いたりする力は教師にしかないことを強調しておく。

● 初めは生徒の不安をなくすために、日本語の魔法がかかっている時間を2～3分の短い時間から始める。

● 次のような、小さい看板 (紙の裏表を使用) を作り、魔法がかかるたびに、使用言語を掲示してもよい。

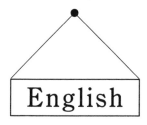

| **45** 俳句を作ろう | ■学習者の<br>　日本語レベル：中級<br><br>■学習者の年齢：11才～18才<br><br>■所要時間：45分 |

## アクティビティのねらい

五七五の音節でリズムとともに主語＋目的語＋述語の語順を学ぶ

### 重要な表現 重要な表現
●特になし

### あらかじめ必要な知識
●助詞の使い方

### 進め方
① 俳句とは何か、俳句の詠み方を説明する。

② 俳句の例を紹介し、五七五の音節構成、主語＋目的語＋述語のつなぎ方、助詞の使い方などの説明をする。

例：

にほんごの　かんじとじょしは　むずかしい

寄せる波　私の足に　ごあいさつ

赤とんぼ　夕やけ空と　同じいろ

見いつけた！　エビのかくれた　さんごしょう

③ 五七五にあてはまり、意味のある句を各自作る。

④ ワークシート (付録参照) に清書する。

⑤ 各自の俳句について説明する。

### 先生方からのアドバイス
●俳句の説明では、季語など俳句の基本的な約束事を説明するが、実際の練習は生徒の日本語のレベルに合わせてルールを決め、やさしく取り組みやすくするとよい。

●上級では、季語や擬態語について学んでも楽しい。

●美術のクラスと共同し、俳画を描くのも面白い (俳画を生徒に紹介し、描かせる)。

●教室展示や句集を作ると生徒のいい思い出となる。

### 付録
●ワークシート

<参考資料>
A Chorus of Haiku.『地球を翔ける俳句の合唱』Jambor, Kinuko A. (Ed.) 1993. Marist Brothers International School. Kobe, Japan. (インターナショナル・スクールの生徒の俳句の作品をまとめたもの)

## 46 読書の木

■学習者の
　日本語レベル：中級、上級

■学習者の年齢：特になし

■所 要 時 間：20分〜40分

### アクティビティのねらい

本を読み、感想文を書くことによって、読書への興味を持たせる

**重要な表現**
- 特になし

**あらかじめ必要な知識**
- 特になし

**準備するもの**
- 縦横15cm程度の木の葉の形をした緑の紙 (付録参照)
- 教室の掲示板に貼る木の幹と枝

**進め方**
① 生徒は本を1冊選んで、読む。
② 読了後、木の葉形の紙に、本の題名と作者、感想、自分の名前を書く。
③ 書き終わったら、クラスで発表する。
④ 発表した木の葉を、掲示板の木の枝につける。

**先生方からのアドバイス**
- 選んだ本が難しすぎると読み終えたという達成感が得られないので、本の選択については教師がアドバイスするとよい。

　**生徒にすすめたい本の例**

　　次のリストは、基本的に小学生を対象としているが、中・高校生の参考にもなるはずである。また、中・高校生には、この他に岩波ジュニア新書シリーズ（岩波書店）などもすすめられる。

　**中級**
　　・キンダーおはなしえほん（フレーベル館）
　　・おはなし絵本館（講談社）
　　・むかしばなしシリーズ（講談社）

　**上級**
　　・日本の名作文庫シリーズ（ポプラ社）
　　・フォア文庫（金の星社）
　　・青い鳥文庫（講談社）

・偕成社文庫（偕成社）

・光村読書シリーズ1年から6年（光村教育図書）

●感想文が書けない場合には、年齢や日本語のレベルに合わせて、アンケートのような用紙を作り、生徒に項目を選択させる形式をとってもよい。

質問項目の例：　　この本は　　1　おもしろかった　　2　つまらなかった
　　　　　　　　　　　　　　　3　長すぎた　　　　　4　短すぎた

**付録**
●木の葉の形をした紙

**47 えんぴつでおしゃべり**

■学習者の
　日本語レベル：中級、上級

■学習者の年齢：特になし

■所 要 時 間：15分〜20分

---

### アクティビティのねらい

お互いに質問し合い、新しい情報を得て、それを文章にまとめる

---

**重要な表現**
- 特になし

**あらかじめ必要な知識**
- 少なくともひらがなを書くこと

**準備するもの**
- ペアごとに1枚ずつのワークシート (付録参照)

**進め方**
① 2人ずつのペアになり、A側とB側 (または生徒のイニシャル、例えばMとOなど
　 としてもよい) を決める (次ページ参照) 。
② 口頭でのおしゃべりは禁止する。
③ その日のテーマを決め、書くことで質問と答えのやりとりを進める。
　 テーマの例: ぼくのペット、きみのペット
　　　　　　　日曜日の予定／日曜日にしたこと
　　　　　　　わたしの家族、あなたの家族
④ やりとりを通じてわかった相手のことを作文にまとめる。

**先生方からのアドバイス**
- 年度初めの最初のクラスなどで行うと、友達作りという意味でも効果的である。
- 一方だけが質問したりすることのないように、ペアの2人が公平に聞いたり、答え
　たりするように促す。
- まとめは短くてもよい。
- ペアごとに書いたものを発表しても楽しい。

**付録**
- ワークシート

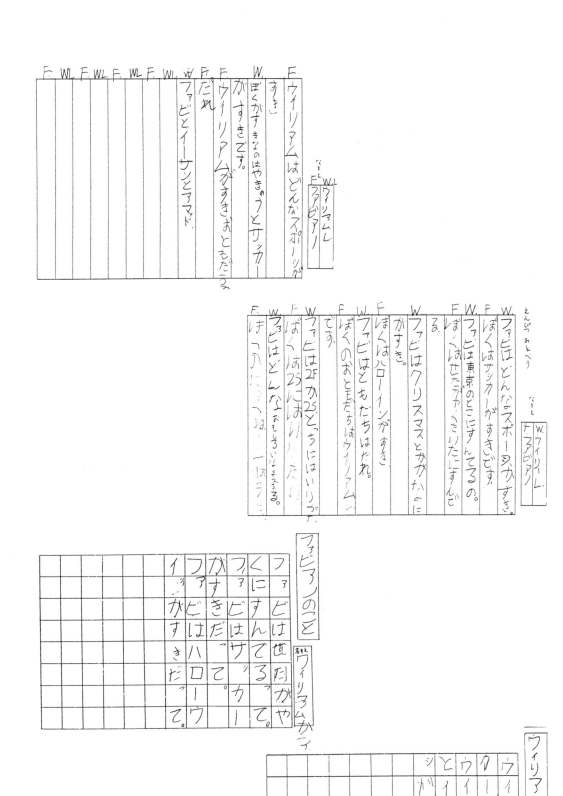

## 48 4コマまんが

■学習者の
　日本語レベル：中級、上級

■学習者の年齢：8才〜18才

■所 要 時 間：45分〜90分

### アクティビティのねらい

会話体の学習、特に話の流れを考えながら話すこと

**重要な表現**
●特になし

**あらかじめ必要な知識**
●話しことばを使った表現

**準備するもの**
●4コマのワークシート
●4コマまんがの例

　　例1:　54. 1.19　　例2:　2. 1.3　　例3: 3. 5. 29　　例4:　2. 7. 17

「フジ三太郎」サトウサンペイ、朝日新聞社

　「2.1.3」は年月日を表し、このまんがが平成2年1月3日に朝日新聞に掲載されたことを示す。また、
「54.1.19」は昭和54年1月19日付けであることを示している。ちなみに、昭和元年は西暦1926年、平成
元年は1989年である。

● OHP (または掲示板)

**進め方**

    ① 4コマまんがの例を見ながら、描かれている人物や事件を確認し、まんがのポイント、時代背景、書かれた視点、おかしみなどを話し合う。

    ② 今学習していることに関連のあるテーマやトピックを選び、まとめ、例、応用のかたちで4つの場面、せりふを考える。

    ③ それを4コマのワークシートに描いていく。特にイラストは興味のある人にまかせてもいいし、共同で、1人が1コマを担当してもよい。

    ④ OHPを使って、または掲示板などにまんがを発表する。

**先生方からのアドバイス**

● 1コマ目をグループに与えて、2、3、4を描かせてもよい。

● 時間のない場合は、せりふのない4コマまんがを使って、せりふだけを書かせることもできる (例1～3参照)。

● クラスの人数や雰囲気によって、ペアワーク、グループワークにするとよい。美術のクラスと共同でのアクティビティにすると楽しい。

● 1コマを1段階とし、4つの段落を作り、せりふではなく筋書きを書くことにしてもよい。

● まんがは、「受験生について」「ことばと社会について」「社会問題について」「家庭の役割について」など、トピックごとに提示してもよい。

&lt;参考資料&gt;

    まんがの例 (コボちゃん、くもんお話カード、サザエさん、フジ三太郎)
    文庫版『サザエさん』45巻　長谷川町子（朝日新聞社　1994～95)
    『対訳サザエさん』12巻　長谷川町子（講談社インターナショナル　1997～）
    文庫版『フジ三太郎名場面』19巻　サトウサンペイ（朝日新聞社　1982～1991）

<table>
<tr><td rowspan="3">**49** よせがき</td><td>■学習者の<br>　日本語レベル：中級、上級</td></tr>
<tr><td>■学習者の年齢：8才〜13才</td></tr>
<tr><td>■所 要 時 間：20分〜45分</td></tr>
</table>

## アクティビティのねらい

決められたテーマについて、短い句や文章を作る

**重要な表現**
- 特になし

**あらかじめ必要な知識**
- 単語または句のレベルで書くこと

**準備するもの**
- 画用紙、色紙など、マーカー、ボールペンなど

**進め方**

① クラス全員で1つのテーマを決める。

　例: 幸せ、家族、朝など

② そのテーマに従って、クラスの全員が書けるように、用紙に記入欄のデザイン (準備するもの参照) をする。

　例:

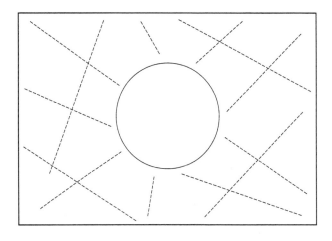

③ 用紙を教室の1ヵ所に置いておき、各自が決められたテーマについて、ひと言書く。いつ書かせるかは、教師が決める。

**先生方からのアドバイス**
- よせがきとは、本来特定の人にあててグループで書くメッセージであり、病院のお見舞い、転校する友達に送るメッセージなどに使われることを話す。年度末に友人同士でお互いにメッセージを書き、送り合うこともできる。

● よせがきの例:

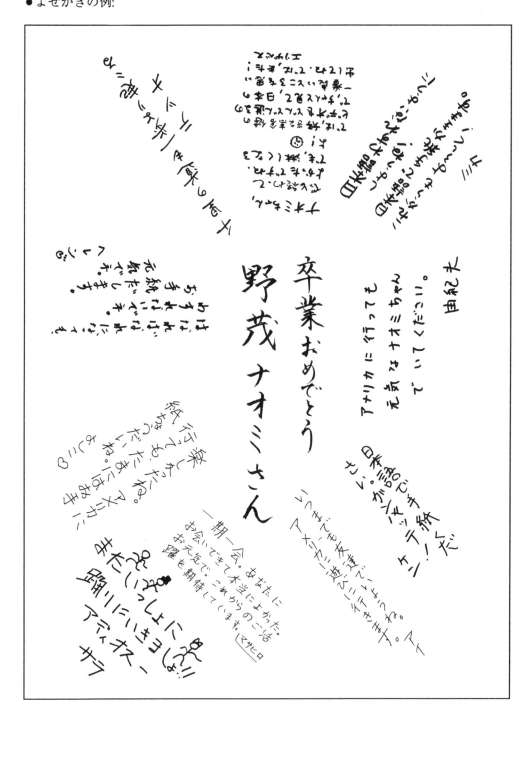

154

# 1枚の紙でできる絵本

## アクティビティのねらい

場面展開によって話の筋を構成する学習をする

## 重要な表現

● 特になし

## あらかじめ必要な知識

● 文章を書くことができる

## 準備するもの

● 画用紙や切り抜き細工用の紙、クレヨン、マーカー、えんぴつ、はさみ、カッターなど
● 下書きの紙
● 参考にするための絵本や絵辞典

## 進め方

① 学習していることの中から、おもしろい事件または人物を取り上げ、クラス全員で話し合う。

② 何人かのグループに分ける。

③ グループごとにテーマをしぼり、その内容を8場面に分ける。

④ 8場面分の作文を下書きする。

⑤ どの場面に絵を入れるか、どんな絵にするかなど、イラストについて相談する。

⑥ ワークシートを次の手順で折る。

　a. 縦に4等分の折り目をつけ、さらに横半分に折る。

　b. 図のように実線の折り目にハサミを入れる。

　c. 切り込みを入れたら、また横半分に折る。

　d. 切り込みを入れたところを図のように左右に開く。

　e. 両端から押し、十字形になったらたたんで小冊子にする。

⑦ 各ページに、お話、絵などをバランスよく配置し、本を作る。

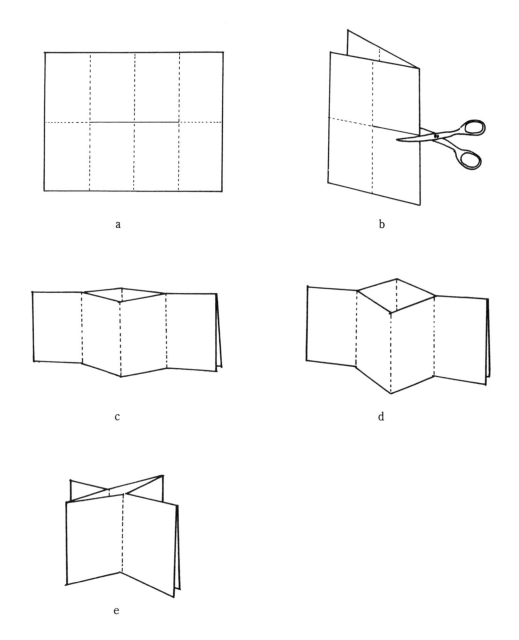

a

b

c

d

e

**先生方からのアドバイス**

● できあがった絵本を掲示したり、ほかのクラスの生徒たちを招いて、読んで聞かせる機会を設けてもよい。

● 各グループで異なったトピックを選択してもよい。

# ❺❶ ニュースの窓

■学習者の日本語レベル：上級

■学習者の年齢：14才～18才

■所 要 時 間：5分～10分

**アクティビティのねらい**

ニュースの内容をまとめて書き、発表して、それを評価する

### 重要な表現

●「～によると、～そうです」

### あらかじめ必要な知識

●テレビ、ラジオの番組のおおよその理解

●新聞、雑誌を読むこと

### 準備するもの

●スピーチ相互評価シート (付録参照)

### 進め方

① 1回の授業につきニュース・キャスターを2人ずつ決める。

② ニュース・キャスターはそれぞれトピックを選び、記事を用意する。

③ 記事をクラスの前で読む。

④ 時間が許せば、クラスで質疑応答をする。

### 先生方からのアドバイス

●トピックは、なるべく新しいものを選ぶようにする。

●このアクティビティは、毎週曜日を定めて、定期的に行うとよい。

●応用として、ニュース・キャスター以外の生徒は、ニュース発表 (ニュース・キャスター) について、評価をし、スピーチ相互評価シートにコメントを書き入れてもよい。

●評価の方法については、内容や例を見せながら、ポイントを示しておくことが必要。批判的なコメントだけでなく、必ず良いコメントを入れることを原則としてもよい。

評価項目例

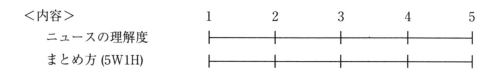

| ＜内容＞ | 1 | 2 | 3 | 4 | 5 |
|---|---|---|---|---|---|
| ニュースの理解度 | | | | | |
| まとめ方 (5W1H) | | | | | |

&lt;発表のしかた&gt;　　　　　　　1　　　　2　　　　3　　　　4　　　　5

ことばがはっきりしている ├─────┼─────┼─────┼─────┤

声が大きくききやすい ├─────┼─────┼─────┼─────┤

語尾まではっきり発音している ├─────┼─────┼─────┼─────┤

話す速度がちょうどよい ├─────┼─────┼─────┼─────┤

&lt;意見&gt;

ニュースの内容や伝え方についての　　　- - - - - - - - - - - - - - - - - - - - - - - - - - - - - -
あなたのコメント

　　　- - - - - - - - - - - - - - - - - - - - - - - - - - - - - -

**付録**　　　- - - - - - - - - - - - - - - - - - - - - - - - - - - - - -

●スピーチ相互評価シート

# INDICES 索引

● **Activities by Level of Japanese** （学習者の日本語レベル）

## Beginners 初級

## All levels すべてのレベル

## Advanced 上級

## Intermediate 中級

## ● Activities by Students' Age （学習者の年齢）

**6 to 8** （6才～8才）

#1    #3    #8

**6 to 10** （6才～10才）

#6    #10    #26
#28   #30

**6 to 13** （6才～13才）

#9    #12    #13
#15   #41

**8 to 10** （8才～10才）

#23   #38

**8 to 13** （8才～13才）

#2    #33    #49

**8 to 18** （8才～18才）

#11   #33    #37
#48   #50

**11 to 13** （11才～13才）

#17

**11 to 18** （11才～18才）

#32   #45    #40

**14 to 18** （14才～18才）

#29   #51

**all** 年齢、特になし

#4    #5    #7    #18
#19   #14   #31   #20
#16   #21   #27   #22
#24   #25   #39   #42
#43   #44   #34   #46
#35   #47   #36

## ● Activities by Time Required （所要時間）

**2 to 3 minutes** （2分～3分）

#15

**5 minutes** （5分）

#1    #8    #23

**5 to 10 minutes** （5分～10分）

#2    #43    #51

**5 to 20 minutes** （5分～20分）

#6

**10 minutes** （10分）

#4 (per category)
#5    #9    #10    #18

**10 to 15 minutes** （10分～15分）

#16   #27    #26

## 15 minutes（15分）

| #3 | #7 | #12 | #20 |
| #22 | #24 | #34 | #36 |

## 30 minutes（30分）

| #28 | #29 | #32 | #33 |

## 15 to 20 minutes（15分～20分）

| #14 | #17 | #21 | #30 |
| #31 | #41 | #47 | |

## 30 to 45 minutes（30分～45分）

#50

## 20 minutes（20分）

| #11 | #13 | #25 |
| #35 | #38 | |

## 45 minutes（45分）

#45

## 20 to 30 minutes（20分～30分）

#40

## 45 to 60 minutes（45分～60分）

#19

## 20 to 40 minutes（20分～40分）

| #42 | #46 |

## 45 to 90 minutes（45分～90分）

| #39 | #48 |

## 20 to 45 minutes（20分～45分）

| #37 | #49 |

## Not applicable（なし）

#44

## ● Activities by Usage　(アクティビティの用途)

| | | WARM-UP (ウォーミング・アップ) | REVIEW (復習) | LESSON (主学習) | GROUPS (小グループ) | WHOLE CLASS (クラス全体) |
|---|---|---|---|---|---|---|
| 1 | Decoding Words (暗号ごっこ) | ● | ● | | | ● |
| 2 | What Color Are the Cards? (何色カード) | ● | ● | | | ● |
| 3 | The Fishing Game (魚釣りゲーム) | | ● | ● | ● | |
| 4 | Making Word Groups (仲間集め) | ● | ● | ● | ● | |
| 5 | Matching Up the Cards (カードあわせ) | ● | ● | | ● | |
| 6 | Win at Cards! (カードで勝負) | | | | ● | |
| 7 | Please Go Straight (まっすぐ行って下さい) | | | | | ● |
| 8 | What's in the Box? (箱の中身は？) | ● | ● | | ● | ● |
| 9 | The Numbers Game (数ゲーム) | ● | ● | | ● | ● |
| 10 | Let's Make Friends (仲間をつくろう) | | | ● | ● | |
| 11 | What Time Is It? (今何時ですか) | | | ● | ● | |
| 12 | The Association Game (連想ゲーム) | | ● | | ● | ● |
| 13 | Put in the Right A, I, U, E, O Order (あいうえお並べ) | | ● | | ● | |
| 14 | Hiragana Scrabble (ひらがなスクラブル) | | ● | ● | ● | |
| 15 | The Way I Am (わたし) | ● | | | | ● |
| 16 | Concentration (神経衰弱) | | ● | | ● | |
| 17 | Gestures (ジェスチャー) | | ● | | ● | ● |
| 18 | Practicing なる (To Become) (「なる」の練習) | | | | ● | ● |
| 19 | Let's Go for a Walk (散歩にいこう) | | | ● | ● | |
| 20 | Do They Sell It or Not? (売っています、売っていません) | | | ● | ● | |
| 21 | What's in the Bag? (袋の中は何でしょう) | | ● | ● | ● | |
| 22 | To Have or Have Not (持っています、持っていません) | | | ● | ● | ● |
| 23 | What's the Odd One Out? (違うものなあに) | ● | ● | | | ● |
| 24 | To Know or Not to Know (知っています、知りません) | | | ● | ● | ● |
| 25 | Crossword Puzzle (クロスワード) | | ● | | ● | ● |

| | | WARM-UP (ウォーミング・アップ) | REVIEW (復習) | LESSON (主学習) | GROUPS (小グループ) | WHOLE CLASS (クラス全体) |
|---|---|---|---|---|---|---|
| 26 | Roulette (ルーレット) | | ● | | ● | |
| 27 | Fukuwarai (福笑い) | | ● | | ● | |
| 28 | The Ice-Cream Shop (アイスクリーム屋さん) | | | ● | ● | ● |
| 29 | What's the Group (何のグループ) | | | ● | ● | ● |
| 30 31 | Sugoroku (数字すごろく、助詞すごろく) | | ● | ● | ● | |
| 32 | When とき, When たら? (〜とき、〜たら) | | | ● | | ● |
| 33 | Department Store (わたしのデパート) | | | ● | ● | |
| 34 | Five-Word Games (作文カードゲーム) | | ● | ● | ● | ● |
| 35 | Which Person Is It? (どの人でしょう) | | | ● | ● | ● |
| 36 | Let's Make Sentences (文を作りましょう) | | ● | ● | ● | |
| 37 | Can You See It? (見えますか？) | | ● | ● | | ● |
| 38 | Make Your Own Menu (メニュー作り) | | | | ● | |
| 39 | Paper Slides (紙スライド) | | | ● | ● | |
| 40 | How about Saturday? (〜曜日はどうですか) | | ● | ● | ● | |
| 41 | The Shopping Game (買い物ゲーム) | | ● | ● | ● | |
| 42 | Bingo (ビンゴ) | | ● | | ● | |
| 43 | Where's the Mistake? (間違いはどこ？) | ● | ● | | | ● |
| 44 | The Magic Word (魔法のことば) | | | | | ● |
| 45 | Let's Write Haiku (俳句を作ろう) | | | | | ● |
| 46 | The Reading Tree (読書の木) | | | | | ● |
| 47 | Pencil Talk (えんぴつでおしゃべり) | | ● | ● | ● | |
| 48 | Comic Strips (4コマまんが) | | | ● | ● | |
| 49 | Yosegaki (よせがき) | | | ● | | ● |
| 50 | Making Picture Books from One Sheet of Paper (1枚の紙でできる絵本) | | | ● | ● | |
| 51 | The News Window (ニュースの窓) | | | | ● | ● |

163

## ❷ What Color Are the Cards?
何色カード

## ❼ Please Go Straight
まっすぐ行って下さい

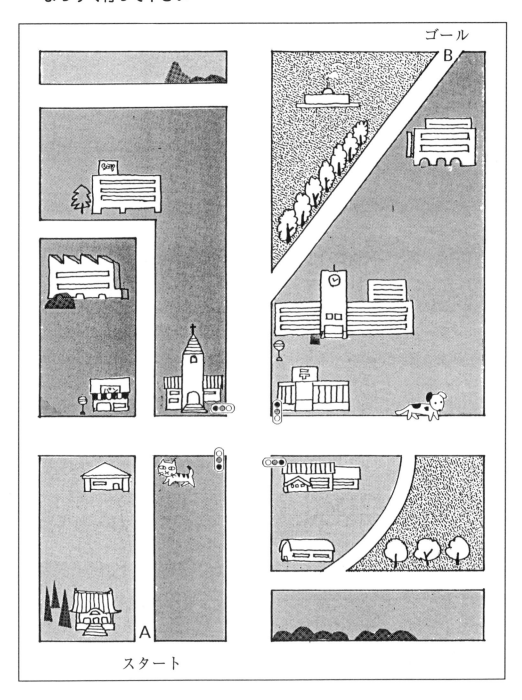

# ⓫ What Time Is It?
## 今何時ですか

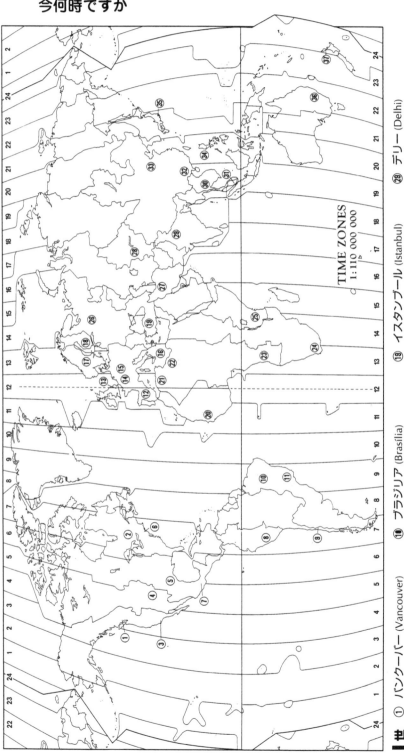

© John Bartholomew & Son Ltd., Edinburgh

TIME ZONES
1:110 000 000

世界の時刻

① バンクーバー (Vancouver)
② トロント (Toronto)
③ ロサンジェルス (Los Angeles)
④ デンバー (Denver)
⑤ ヒューストン (Houston)
⑥ ニューヨーク (New York)
⑦ メキシコ・シティー (Mexico City)
⑧ リマ (Lima)
⑨ サンティアゴ (Santiago)

⑩ ブラジリア (Brasília)
⑪ リオ・デ・ジャネイロ (Rio de Janeiro)
⑫ マドリッド (Madrid)
⑬ ロンドン (London)
⑭ パリ (Paris)
⑮ フランクフルト (Frankfurt)
⑯ ローマ (Rome)
⑰ ストックホルム (Stockholm)
⑱ ヘルシンキ (Helsinki)

⑲ イスタンブール (Istanbul)
⑳ ダカール (Dakar)
㉑ アルジェ (Algiers)
㉒ トリポリ (Tripoli)
㉓ ルアンダ (Luanda)
㉔ ケープ・タウン (Cape Town)
㉕ ナイロビ (Nairobi)
㉖ モスクワ (Moscow)
㉗ テヘラン (Teheran)
㉘ タシュケント (Tashkent)

㉙ デリー (Delhi)
㉚ バンコク (Bangkok)
㉛ クアラ・ルンプール (Kuala Lumpur)
㉜ ハノイ (Hanoi)
㉝ 北京 (ペキン) (Beijing)
㉞ マニラ (Manila)
㉟ 東京 (トウキョウ) (Tokyo)
㊱ シドニー (Sydney)
㊲ オークランド (Auckland)

167

## ⓮ Hiragana Scrabble
### ひらがなスクラブル

**⑲ Let's Go for a Walk**
散歩にいこう

なまえ ＿＿＿＿＿＿＿＿＿＿

| | | |
|---|---|---|
| あ＿＿＿＿＿ | た＿＿＿＿＿ | ま＿＿＿＿＿ |
| い＿＿＿＿＿ | ち＿＿＿＿＿ | み＿＿＿＿＿ |
| う＿＿＿＿＿ | つ＿＿＿＿＿ | む＿＿＿＿＿ |
| え＿＿＿＿＿ | て＿＿＿＿＿ | め＿＿＿＿＿ |
| お＿＿＿＿＿ | と＿＿＿＿＿ | も＿＿＿＿＿ |
| か＿＿＿＿＿ | な＿＿＿＿＿ | や＿＿＿＿＿ |
| き＿＿＿＿＿ | に＿＿＿＿＿ | |
| く＿＿＿＿＿ | ぬ＿＿＿＿＿ | ゆ＿＿＿＿＿ |
| け＿＿＿＿＿ | ね＿＿＿＿＿ | |
| こ＿＿＿＿＿ | の＿＿＿＿＿ | よ＿＿＿＿＿ |
| さ＿＿＿＿＿ | は＿＿＿＿＿ | ら＿＿＿＿＿ |
| し＿＿＿＿＿ | ひ＿＿＿＿＿ | り＿＿＿＿＿ |
| す＿＿＿＿＿ | ふ＿＿＿＿＿ | る＿＿＿＿＿ |
| せ＿＿＿＿＿ | へ＿＿＿＿＿ | れ＿＿＿＿＿ |
| そ＿＿＿＿＿ | ほ＿＿＿＿＿ | ろ＿＿＿＿＿ |

## ⑳ Do They Sell It or Not?
売っています、売っていません

| 店の名前 ＼ 品 名 | | | |
|---|---|---|---|
| | | | |
| | | | |
| | | | |

## ㉒ To Have or Have Not
持っています、持っていません

| 名 前 ＼ 品 名 | | | |
|---|---|---|---|
| | | | |
| | | | |
| | | | |

## ㉔ To Know or Not to Know
知っています、知りません

| 名 前 ＼ 項 目 | | | |
|---|---|---|---|
| | | | |
| | | | |
| | | | |

## ㉕ Crossword Puzzle
クロスワード

あいさつのことば

| | | | | | | | | |
|---|---|---|---|---|---|---|---|---|
| よ | い | こ | ん | ば | ん | は | が | あ |
| ご | め | ん | な | さ | い | と | り | い |
| ち | ん | に | ら | さ | お | が | い | た |
| そ | は | ち | う | よ | と | や | え | だ |
| う | お | は | よ | う | な | さ | す | い |
| さ | あ | り | が | な | ま | し | い | み |
| ま | す | か | は | ら | す | え | ら | な |

教室にあるもの

| | | | | | | |
|---|---|---|---|---|---|---|
| え | ん | ぴ | お | の | う | か |
| ほ | の | り | が | み | と | み |
| さ | が | つ | く | け | は | ご |
| み | は | み | い | す | し | さ |
| と | ほ | さ | え | ん | ぴ | つ |
| ん | ま | く | み | し | み | く |
| て | け | し | ご | む | き | え |

えとの動物

| か | み | い | ま | は | つ | う | な | は | へ |
|---|---|---|---|---|---|---|---|---|---|
| に | ら | り | み | す | し | さ | わ | ね | ぬ |
| き | と | ら | あ | な | う | ぎ | お | ん | に |
| な | く | か | け | さ | く | ら | ね | さ | た |
| れ | く | ふ | い | せ | そ | ず | へ | の | ひ |
| こ | ひ | へ | ぬ | の | み | び | ん | ま | つ |
| は | た | が | い | ま | し | ら | さ | と | じ |
| あ | ほ | つ | や | ね | う | し | る | り | ら |
| ろ | ま | う | ず | ず | ま | へ | ま | こ | え |
| な | う | し | え | み | こ | け | も | う | も |

```
よ い こ ん ば ん は が あ
ご め ん な さ い と り い
ち ん に ら さ お が い た
そ は ち う よ と や え だ
う お は よ う な さ す い
さ あ り が な ま し い み
ま す か は ら す え ら な
```

```
え ん ぴ お の う か み
ほ の り が み と み
さ が つ け は ご
み は み い す し さ
と ほ さ え ん ぴ つ
ん ま く み し み く
て け し ご む き え
```

```
か み い ま は つ う な は へ
に ら り み す し さ わ ね ぬ
き と ら あ な う ぎ お ん に
な く か け さ く ら ね さ た
れ く ふ い せ そ ず へ の ひ
こ ひ へ ぬ の み び ん ま つ
は た が い ま し ら さ と じ
あ ほ つ や ね う し る り ら
ろ ま ん ず ず ま へ ま こ え
な う し え み こ け も う も
```

## ㉖ **Roulette**
ルーレット

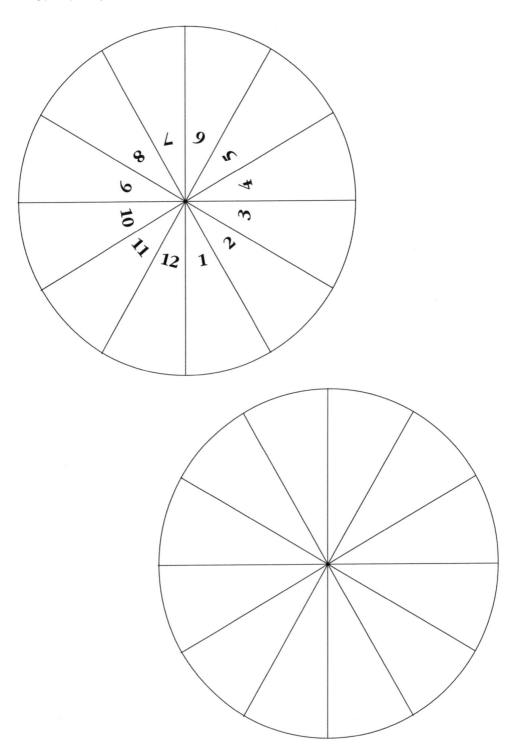

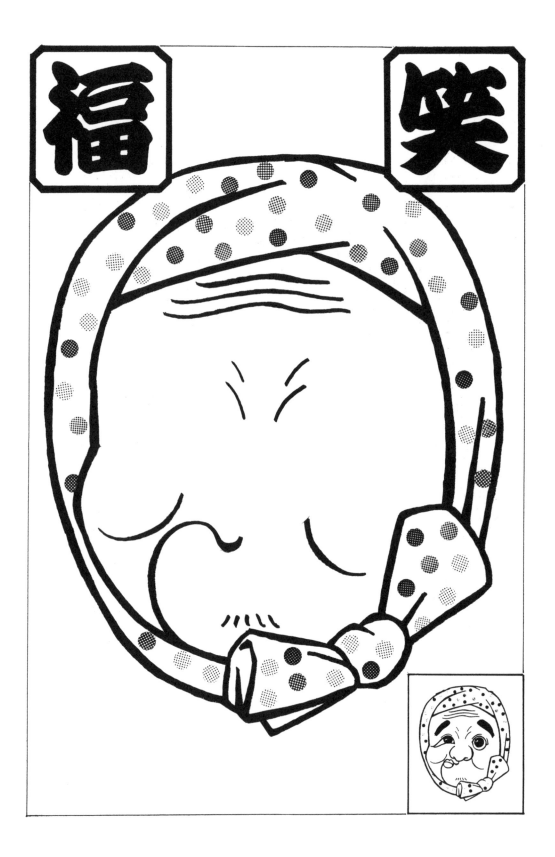

## ㉚ Sugoroku with Numbers
数字すごろく

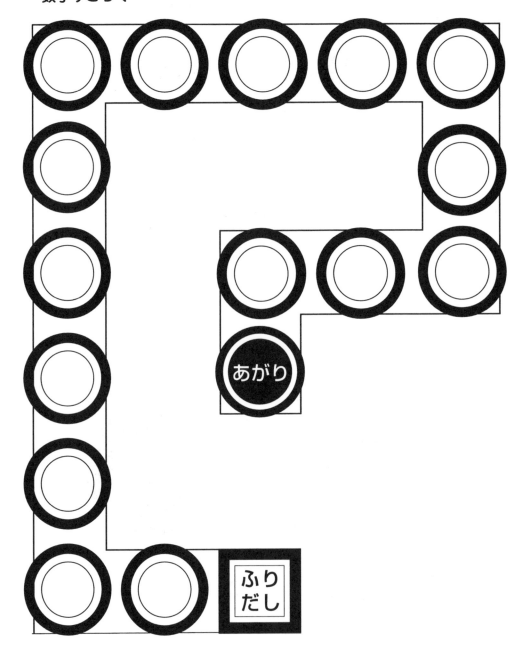

## ㉛ Sugoroku with Particles
助詞すごろく

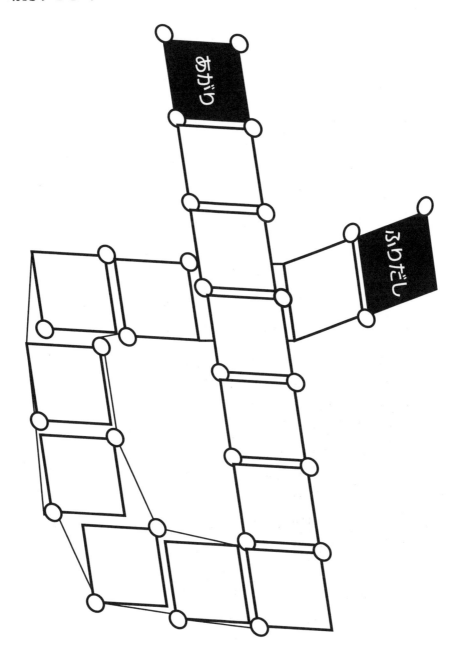

## ㉝ Department Store
わたしのデパート

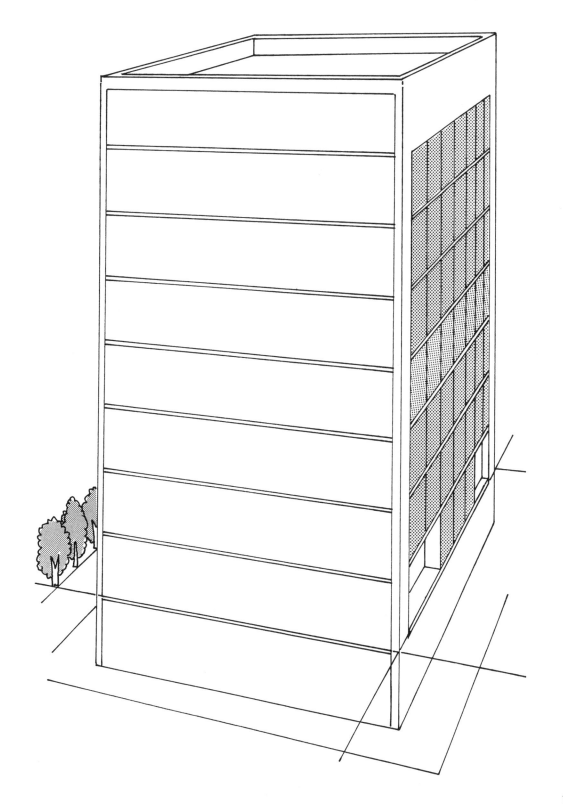

# ㊲ Can You See It?
見えますか？

**EYE TEST FORM** 視力表

けんさ日　　平成　　年　月　日

名　前　＿＿＿＿＿＿＿＿＿＿＿

|  | 左目 | 右目 |
|---|---|---|
| 視力 |  |  |

## 観察

＿＿＿＿＿＿＿＿＿＿＿＿＿＿＿＿＿＿＿＿＿＿＿＿＿＿

＿＿＿＿＿＿＿＿＿＿＿＿＿＿＿＿＿＿＿＿＿＿＿＿＿＿

＿＿＿＿＿＿＿＿＿＿＿＿＿＿＿＿＿＿＿＿＿＿＿＿＿＿

＿＿＿＿＿＿＿＿＿＿＿＿＿＿＿＿＿＿＿＿＿＿＿＿＿＿

**EYE CHART** 視力検査表

| | | | | | |
|---|---|---|---|---|---|
| ○ | 4 | に | | | 0.1 |
| ○ | ○ | 2 | け | リ | 0.2 |
| C | ○ | 4 | い | さ | 0.3 |
| ○ | C | 2 | こ | つ | 0.4 |
| ○ | C | 4 | に | く | 0.5 |
| ○ | ○ | 1 | い | け | 0.6 |
| ○ | ○ | 7 | へ | て | 0.7 |
| ○ | ○ | ロ | つ | へ | 0.8 |
| C | ○ | 1 | い | こ | 0.9 |
| ○ | ○ | 4 | に | い | 1.0 |
| ○ | ○ | 7 | け | リ | 1.2 |
| ○ | ○ | ロ | へ | に | 1.5 |
| c | ○ | 1 | リ | こ | 2.0 |

The eye chart should be enlarged until the big circle in the upper left corner has a diameter of 45 mm. The chart should be viwed form a distance of 3 meters.

一番大きい輪（上段左）の直径が45mmになるまで拡大コピーし、3mはなれてまっすぐ見て下さい。

183

## ⓴ How about Saturday?
### ～曜日はどうですか

|  | 8:00 | 9:00 | 10:00 | 11:00 | 12:00 | 1:00 | 2:00 | 3:00 | 4:00 | 5:00 | 6:00 | 7:00 | 8:00 | 9:00 | 10:00 |
|---|---|---|---|---|---|---|---|---|---|---|---|---|---|---|---|
| ／ 日 | | | | | | | | | | | | | | | |
| ／ 月 | | | | | | | | | | | | | | | |
| ／ 火 | | | | | | | | | | | | | | | |
| ／ 水 | | | | | | | | | | | | | | | |
| ／ 木 | | | | | | | | | | | | | | | |
| ／ 金 | | | | | | | | | | | | | | | |
| ／ 土 | | | | | | | | | | | | | | | |

## 45 Let's Write Haiku
俳句を作ろう

なまえ

## ㊽ The Reading Tree
読書の木

本の題名

作者

感想

名前

## ❹ Pencil Talk
えんぴつでおしゃべり

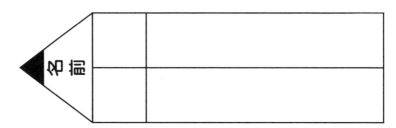

|  |  |
|---|---|
|  |  |
|  |  |
|  |  |
|  |  |
|  |  |
|  |  |
|  |  |
|  |  |
|  |  |
|  |  |

## (51) The News Window
## ニュースの窓

| ＜内容＞ | 1 | 2 | 3 | 4 | 5 |
|---|---|---|---|---|---|
| ニュースの理解度 | | | | | |
| まとめ方 (5W1H) | | | | | |

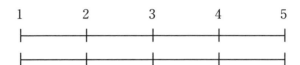

| ＜発表のしかた＞ | 1 | 2 | 3 | 4 | 5 |
|---|---|---|---|---|---|
| ことばがはっきりしている | | | | | |
| 声が大きくききやすい | | | | | |
| 語尾まではっきり発音している | | | | | |
| 話す速度がちょうどよい | | | | | |

＜意見＞

ニュースの内容や伝え方についての
あなたのコメント

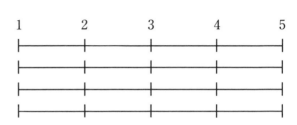

日本語教材・アクティビティ集
BITS AND PIECES

1997年 8 月11日　第 1 刷発行

著　者　　日本インターナショナルスクール協議会

発行者　　野間佐和子

発行所　　講談社インターナショナル株式会社
　　　　　〒112 東京都文京区音羽 1-17-14
　　　　　電話：03-3944-6493

印刷所　　株式会社　平河工業社

製本所　　株式会社　国宝社

MRS. K. M. PRIEST
81 BEAUMONT ROAD
CAMBRIDGE CB1 4PX